BACKPAY

Tamantha Hammerschlag

The Royal Court Writers Series
published by Methuen Drama
in association with the Royal Court Theatre

Methuen Drama

Royal Court Writers Series

First published in Great Britain in the
Royal Court Writers Series in 1997
by Methuen Drama

ISBN 0 413 71760 7

A CIP catalogue record for this book is available
at the British Library

Typeset by Country Setting, Woodchurch, Kent TN26 3TB

The Royal Court 1996 Young Writers' Festival
presents

BACKPAY

by Tamantha Hammerschlag

First performance at the Royal Court Theatre Upstairs
Stage Space 29 October 1996
(as part of the Royal Court/Marks & Spencer Young Writers' Festival 1996).

First performance at the Royal Court Theatre Upstairs
Circle Space 6 February 1997.

An Eastern Touring Agency Initiative in association
with the Royal Court Theatre.

The Royal Court Theatre is financially assisted by the Royal Borough of
Kensington and Chelsea. Recipient of a grant from the Theatre Restoration
Fund & from the Foundation for Sport & the Arts. The Royal Court's Play
Development Programme is funded by the Audrey Skirball-Kenis Theatre.
Supported by the National Lottery through the Arts Council of England.
Royal Court Registered Charity number 231242.

The English Stage Company at the Royal Court Theatre

The English Stage Company was formed to bring serious writing back to the stage. The first Artistic Director, George Devine, wanted to create a vital and popular theatre. He encouraged new writing that explored subjects drawn from contemporary life as well as pursuing European plays and forgotten classics. When John Osborne's **Look Back in Anger** was first produced in 1956, it forced British Theatre into the modern age. In addition to plays by "angry young men", the international repertoire ranged from Brecht to Ionesco, by way of Jean-Paul Sartre, Marguerite Duras, Wedekind and Beckett.

The ambition was to discover new work which was challenging, innovative and also of the highest quality, underpinned by the desire to discover a contemporary style of presentation. Early Court writers included Arnold Wesker, John Arden, David Storey, Ann Jellicoe, N F Simpson and Edward Bond. They were followed by David Hare and Howard Brenton, Caryl Churchill, Timberlake Wertenbaker, Robert Holman and Jim Cartwright. Many of their plays are now regarded as modern classics.

Many established playwrights had their early plays produced in the Theatre Upstairs including Anne Devlin, Andrea Dunbar, Sarah Daniels, Jim Cartwright, Clare McIntyre, Winsome Pinnock, Martin Crimp and Phyllis Nagy. Since 1994 there has been a major season of plays by writers new to the Royal Court, many of them first plays, produced in association with the *Royal National Theatre Studio* with sponsorship from *The Jerwood Foundation*. The writers include Joe Penhall, Nick Grosso, Judy Upton, Sarah Kane, Michael Wynne, Judith Johnson, James Stock, Simon Block and Mark Ravenhill. In 1996-97 The Jerwood Foundation sponsored the Jerwood New Playwrights season, a series of six plays by Jez Butterwoth and Martin McDonagh (in the Theatre Downstairs), Mark Ravenhill, Ayub Khan-Din, Tamantha Hammerschlag and Jess Walters (in the Theatre Upstairs).

Theatre Upstairs productions have regularly transferred to the Theatre Downstairs, as with Ariel Dorfman's **Death and the Maiden**, Sebastian Barry's **The Steward of Christendom**, a co-production with *Out of Joint*, and Martin McDonagh's **The Beauty Queen Of Leenane,** a co-production with Druid Theatre Company. Some Theatre Upstairs productions have transferred to the West End, most recently with Kevin Elyot's **My Night With Reg** at the Criterion. 1992-1996 have been record-breaking years at the box-office with capacity houses for productions of **Faith Healer, Death and the Maiden, Six Degrees of Separation, King Lear, Oleanna, Hysteria, Cavalcaders, The Kitchen, The Queen & I, The Libertine, Simpatico, Mojo** and **The Steward of Christendom**.

Death and the Maiden and **Six Degrees of Separation** won the Olivier Award for Best Play in 1992 and 1993 respectively. **Hysteria** won the 1994 Olivier Award for Best Comedy, and also the Writers' Guild Award for Best West End Play. **My Night with Reg** won the 1994 Writers' Guild Award for Best Fringe Play, the Evening Standard Award for Best Comedy, and the 1994 Olivier Award for Best Comedy. Jonathan Harvey won the 1994 Evening Standard Drama Award for Most Promising Playwright, for **Babies**. Sebastian Barry won the 1995 Writers' Guild Award for Best Fringe Play for **The Steward of Christendom** and also the 1995 Lloyds Private Banking Playwright of the Year Award. Jez Butterworth won the 1995 George Devine Award for Most Promising Playwright, the 1995 Writers' Guild New Writer of the Year, the Evening Standard Award for Most Promising Newcomer and the 1995 Olivier Award for Best Comedy for **Mojo**. Phyllis Nagy won the 1995 Writers' Guild Award for Best Regional Play for **Disappeared**. Martin McDonagh won the 1996 George Devine Award for Most Promising Playwright, the 1996 Writers' Guild Best Fringe Play Award, and the 1996 Evening Standard Drama Award for Most Promising Newcomer for **The Beauty Queen of Leenane**. The Royal Court won the 1995 Prudential Award for the Theatre, and was the overall winner of the 1995 Prudential Award for the Arts for creativity, excellence, innovation and accessibility. The Royal Court won the 1995 Peter Brook Empty Space Award for innovation and excellence in theatre.

Now in its temporary homes The Duke Of York's and Ambassadors Theatres, during the two-year refurbishment of its Sloane Square theatre, the Royal Court continues to present the best in new work. After four decades the company's aims remain consistent with those established by George Devine. The Royal Court is still a major focus in the country for the production of new work. Scores of plays first seen at the Royal Court are now part of the national and international dramatic repertoire.

Welcome to this performance of **Backpay**, an initiative between *Eastern Touring Agency* and the Royal Court for small scale theatres and arts centres in the East of England This tour is the culmination of a 3 year relationship between *Eastern Touring Agency* and the Royal Court. *Eastern Touring Agency*, in partnership with our 25 strong network of small scale venues, is working to provide you, our audience, with the best the performing arts has to offer.

By commissioning and touring all kinds of performing arts events and by surrounding these tours with effective educational and marketing support, we try to encourage first time theatregoers and make sure that everyone, wherever they are in the East of England, has the opportunity to give the arts a go. So, if this is your first visit to this theatre, we extend an especially warm welcome to you.

If you saw *Sweetheart*, last year's collaboration between *Eastern Touring Agency* and the Royal Court Theatre, welcome back! I am sure you will agree that **Backpay**, a wonderful play by another new young writer, is just as enjoyable as *Sweetheart*.

Thank you to the Royal Court for their dedication to the task of creating theatre for intimate spaces and for the total commitment of the education and marketing teams to the project.

Lynne Williams
Artistic Director
Eastern Touring Agency

For the past three years the Royal Court has toured new plays to the East of England. We are delighted that over this period the relationship with *Eastern Touring Agency* and our host theatre has been so productive . We would also like to thank the **Paul Hamlyn Foundation** who have also supported the work, particularly funding the workshop programme (aimed at young people between the ages of 16 and 25) and so encouraging continuing audiences for theatre into the next century.

Dominic Tickell
Director
Royal Court Young People's Theatre

BACKPAY is produced by the Royal Court Young People's Theatre.

Producer Dominic Tickell
Tour Administrator Aoife Mannix
Press Cameron Duncan PR
Tel: 0171-383 0866
Fax: 0171-388 0419

At the Royal Court Theatre Downstairs
St.Martin's Lane WC2

The Royal Court Theatre presents
From 13 February

THE SHALLOW END

by Doug Lucie

At the Royal Court Theatre Upstairs
West St WC2

The Royal Court Theatre presents
Until 1 March
Stage

COCKROACH, WHO?

by Jess Walters

The Royal Court Theatre presents
From 7 March

ATTEMPTS ON HER LIFE

by Martin Crimp

8 - 12 April

VOICES FROM SPAIN

A week of new plays, translated into English, from Spanish and Catalan.

JERWOOD
NEW PLAYWRIGHTS

Jerwood New Playwrights sees the Jerwood Foundation coming forward for a second year as a major sponsor of the Royal Court Theatre. This series of six plays staged in the winter and spring of 1996-7, is a notable celebration of the best of contemporary playwriting. Certain of the plays reached the Royal Court stage last year, to great acclaim - **Mojo** by Jez Butterworth and **The Beauty Queen of Leenane** by Martin McDonagh. The fact that others are new plays underlines still further the notable importance of the Royal Court as a forcing ground for new talent.

I am a great admirer of the exceptionally high artistic level the Royal Court has achieved. This achievement fits perfectly with the ideals of the Jerwood Foundation, a private foundation established in 1977 by the late John Jerwood. It is dedicated to imaginative and responsible funding and sponsorship of the arts, education, design, conservation, medicine, science and engineering, and of other areas of human endeavour and excellence.

The Foundation is increasingly known for its support of the arts. In the field of the visual arts, two major awards are increasingly bringing it to public attention. The first is the Jerwood Painting Prize, now in its third year and the most valuable art prize in the United Kingdom. The second is the Jerwood Foundation Prize for Applied Arts, the largest prize of its kind in Europe, which in 1996 was offered for ceramics.

The Council of the Foundation has singled out one particular strand for development within the Foundation's varied field of benefactors: support of talented young people who have persevered in their chosen career and will benefit from the financial support and recognition which will launch them. To achieve this goal, a number of awards and sponsorships have been developed in concert with organisations such as the Royal Ballet Companies (for the Jerwood Young Choreographers Awards); the National Film and Television School; the Royal Academy of Dancing; and the Royal Academy of Engineering.

The Foundation sponsors the Brereton International Music Symposium which gives masterclasses for young professional windplayers and singers, the National Youth Chamber Orchestra, and the Opera and Music Theatre Lab at Bore Place in Kent. In 1996, with The Big Issue it co-sponsored The Big Screening , a free season of new films by British directors. Across all the arts, it is vital that financial support is given to the creation of new work. It is for this simple reason that we are delighted to be sponsoring another exciting season with the Royal Court.

Alan Grieve
Chairman

BACKPAY

by Tamantha Hammerschlag

Sophie	*Doña Croll*
Mother	*Leda Hodgson*
Adele	*Valerie Hunkins*
Mina	*Diane O'Kelly*
Bafana	*Shaun Parkes*

Director	Mary Peate
Designer	Tom Piper
Lighting Designer	Matthew O'Connor
Sound Designer	Fergus O'Hare
Production Manager	Paul Handley
Senior Stage Manager	Maris Sharp
Stage Managers	Susannah Rigby
	Trace Roberts-Shaw
Costume Supervisor	Iona Kenrick
Tour Manager	Craig Becker
Fight Director	Terry King
Dialect Coach	Joan Washington

The Royal Court would like to thank the following for their help with this production: Cover image - photo of Celeste MacIlwaine; Harvey Furnishings Group; Menthol Cigarettes donated by Honey Products Ltd, Stowmarket; Habitat UK; Streatham Library; Matress supplied by Beaumont Beds Ltd 0181 853 115; Dairy Crest Dairies; Greenwich Bread and Cake Company; Mr Kipling Cakes, Manor Bakeries; Greyfiars Bakeries; Wardrobe care by Persil and Comfort courtesy of Lever Brothers Ltd, refrigerators by Electrolux and Philips Major Appliances Ltd.; kettles for rehearsals by Morphy Richards; video for casting purposes by Hitachi; backstage coffee machine by West 9; furniture by Knoll International; freezer for backstage use supplied by Zanussi Ltd 'Now that's a good idea.' Hair styling by Carole at Moreno, 2 Holbein Place, Sloane Square 0171-730- 0211; Closed circuit TV cameras and monitors by Mitsubishi UK Ltd. Natural spring water from Wye Spring Water, 149 Sloane Street, London SW1, tel. 0171-730 6977. Overhead projector from W.H. Smith; Sanyo U.K for the backstage microwave.

Tamantha Hammerschlag (writer)

Tamantha Hammerschlag is 23 years old, and is from Edenvale in South Africa. She studied Drama and English at the University of the Witwartesrand, before completing an M.A in Theatre Studies at Royal Holloway, University of London, where she studied scriptwriting under Winsome Pinnock. She has previously written three plays, which were staged at the Grahamstown Festival in South Africa.

Doña Croll

For the Royal Court: God's Second in Command, Basin, A Mouthful of Birds, The Burrow, Mohair (Young Writers Festival 1987), Serious Money (Wyndhams).
Other theatre includes: Nine Night, Gin Trap (Bush); Jericho (Young Vic); The Old Order (Birmingham Rep); Jelly Roll Soul, The Relapse (Lyric Hammersmith); It's a Mad House (Crucible Sheffield); Polly, Back to Methusalah (Cambridge Theatre Company); Golden Girls (West Yorkshire Playhouse); Hansel and Gretel, No Boy's Cricket Club (Stratford East); The Merchant of Venice (Royal Exchange); Othello, The City Wives Confederacy (Greenwich); Joe Turner's Come and Gone,

Victor and the Ladies (Tricycle); Antony and Cleopatra (Talawa). Television includes: The Boys from the Blackstuff; Nation's Health, Come to Mecca, 6 O'Clock Show, Black Silk, Ebony, Some Day Man, EastEnders, The Real Eddy English, The Paradise Club, Troublemakers, The Bill, Hallelujah Anyhow, Rides, Surgical Spirit, Desmonds, Us Girls, Between the Lines, Casualty, Birds of a Feather, Chandler and Co, Loving Hazel, Brothers and Sisters.

Leda Hodgson

For the Royal Court: Storming (Young Writers' Festival 1996); The Terrible Voice of Satan. Other theatre includes: A Midsummer Night's Dream, The Man of Mode (Cheek by Jowl); Shakers (Hull Truck); A Small Family Business (Birmingham Rep); The Normal Heart (Harrogate); Tons of Money (Derby Playhouse); The Dramatic Attitudes of Miss Fanny Kemble, Man of the Moment (Swan, Worcester); The Wizard of Oz (Everyman, Liverpool); Jane Eyre (Everyman, Cheltenham); No Fond Return of Love (Man in the Moon); Once a Catholic (Coliseum, Oldham); The Norman Conquests (Salisbury Playhouse); Wildest Dreams (Library Theatre, Manchester); Happy Families (Watford).

Television includes: Take Three Women, After the Dance, Meat, Hamish Macbeth.

Valerie Hunkins

For the Royal Court: Storming (Young Writers' Festival 1996); God's Second in Command. Other theatre includes: Romeo and Juliet (West 28th St. Theatre Co.); The Investigation (Duke's Head); Simon Boccanegra, La Bohème (ENO); The Singing Ringing Tree (Contact, Manchester); Peer Gynt, Racing Demon, Magic Carpet (RNT), Fatherland (Riverside Studios); Moon on a Rainbow Shawl (Almeida); Zebra Days (Resisters Theatre Co.); Tiger Fly (Umoja Theatre); The ABC Show, Destination Unknown (Salamander Theatre Co.); The Rush (Roots Theatre).
Television includes: Raffle Baby, Casualty, Come Outside, Just Us, Us Girls, Gallowglass, The Bill, Conspiracy of Cells, A Sense of Guilt, Hardcases, Hyperspace Hotel, Urban Habitat. Film includes: Ladybird, Ladybird.

Matthew O'Connor (lighting)

For the Royal Court: Storming (Young Writers' Festival 1996); Never Mind the Ballot Box, A Report to an Academy. Other theatre and concert lighting designs include: The Queen and I (Theatre of Comedy); Fifth of July

(Bristol Old Vic); Arsenic and Old Lace, Blue Eyed Boy, The Odd Couple, Images of Love (Liverpool Playhouse); Legends of Evil, Fear and Misery of the Third Reich/Fears and Miseries of the Third Term (Altered States Theatre Co.); As You Like It (Devon Shakespeare Project); Gilbert O'Sullivan (British tour); Man to Man (Man in the Moon); Now We are Free, The Rape When No Means... (Edinburgh Fringe 1995); The Pigeon Banquet (Watermans); Anoraknaphobia (Link Theatre.)

Fergus O'Hare (sound)
For the Royal Court: Storming (Young Writers' Festival 1996); Mules. Other theatre includes: Miss Julie (Young Vic); Keyboard Skills (Bush); September Tide (Kings Head/Comedy); The King and I (Covent Garden Festival); The Life of Stuff, Glengarry Glen Ross, True West, Maria Friedman by Special Arrangement, Endgame, Habeas Corpus (Donmar Warehouse); Shakuntala (Gate).

Diane O'Kelly
For the Royal Court: Storming (Young Writers' Festival 1996); Other theatre includes: The Seal Wife (Stellar Quines Theatre Co tour); At the Black Pig's Dyke (Druid Theatre Co. tour, Tricycle Theatre, Mayfest, Toronto, Australian tour); The Snow Queen (Hull Truck Theatre Co.) Television includes: Soldier Soldier, The Bill, Cracker, O Mary this London, Jackanory. Film includes: Ailsa. Radio includes: Children of the Dead End, Along a Lonely Road, After Easter.

Shaun Parkes
Graduated RADA June 1994.
For the Royal Court: Storming (Young Writers' Festival 1996).
Other theatre includes: The Duchess of Malfi (Wyndhams); Life and Death of a Buffalo Soldier (Bristol Old Vic); Romeo and Juliet (Stephen Joseph, Scarborough). Television includes: Turning World, Heartbeat, Crown Prosecutor, Soldier Solider, Casualty, Degrees of Error.

Mary Peate (director)
For the Royal Court: Backpay (Young Writers' Festival 1996), Waiting Room Germany.
As Assistant Director: The Beauty Queen of Leenane; Oleanna (and Duke of York's); Hammett's Apprentice, The Treatment. Other theatre includes: Grave Dancer (Finborough); Picnic, Guernica (Gate). She was Artistic Director of the Finborough Theatre, and Assistant Director at the Gate Theatre, Notting Hill.

Tom Piper (design)
For the Royal Court: Storming (Young Writers' Festival 1996).
Design for theatre includes: Much Ado About Nothing, A Patriot for Me, Spring Awakening, The Broken Heart (RSC); Blinded by the Sun, The Birthday Party (RNT); Kindertransport (Palace, Watford and Vaudeville); Six Characters in Search of an Author, The Crucible (Abbey Theatre, Dublin); Sweet Panic, The Philanderer (Hampstead); Endgame, Dumbstruck, Macbeth, Cinderella, Jack and the Beanstalk (Tron Theatre); The Duchess of Malfi (Greenwich and West End); Tulip Futures, My Goat, Ripped, Kindertransport, The Rock Station (Soho Theatre Co.); Sacred Hearts (Communicado Theatre); The Master Builder (Royal Lyceum, Edinburgh); Golem (Northern Stage Company and Northern Sinfonia); The Price (York Theatre Royal); The Way of the World, No One Writes to the Colonel (Lyric Hammersmith); The Masked Ball (Dublin Grand Opera); The Cherry Orchard (Nottingham Playhouse); The Dark River, Cat with Green Violin, His Majesty, Mrs Warren's Profession, We the Undersigned (Orange Tree); La Chunga, The Healer (Old Red Lion); A Cat in the Ghetto (Tabard Theatre); Noyes Flude (St James Church and Albert Hall).
Opera includes: Golem (Northern Stage Opera).

Share more fully in the life of the Royal Court by joining our supporters and investing in New Theatre

Call: 0171-930-4253

Many thanks to all our supporters for their vital and on-going commitment

How the Royal Court is brought to you

The Royal Court (English Stage Company Ltd) is supported financially by a wide range of public bodies and private companies, as well as its own trading activities. The company receives its principal funding from the **Arts Council of England**, which has supported the Royal Court since 1956. The **Royal Borough of Kensington & Chelsea** gives an annual grant to the Royal Court Young People's Theatre and provides some of its staff. The **London Boroughs Grants Committee** contributes to the cost of productions in the Theatre Upstairs.

Other parts of the company's activities are made possible by business sponsorships. Several of these sponsors have made a long-term commitment. 1996 saw the sixth Barclays New Stages Festival of Independent Theatre, supported throughout by **Barclays Bank**. **British Gas North Thames** supported three years of the Royal Court's Education Programme. Sponsorship by **WH Smith** helped to make the launch of the Friends of the Royal Court scheme so successful.

1993 saw the start of our association with the **Audrey Skirball-Kenis Theatre** of Los Angeles, which is funding a Playwrights Programme at the Royal Court. Exchange visits for writers between Britain and the USA complement the greatly increased programme of readings and workshops which have fortified the company's capability to develop new plays.

In 1988 the **Olivier Building Appeal** was launched, to raise funds to begin the task of restoring, repairing and improving the Royal Court Theatre, Sloane Square. This was made possible by a large number of generous supporters and significant contributions from the **Theatres Restoration Fund**, the **Rayne Foundation**, the **Foundation for Sport and the Arts** and the **Arts Council's Incentive Funding Scheme**.

The Company earns the rest of the money it needs to operate from the Box Office, from other trading and from transfers to the West End of plays such as **Death and the Maiden**, **Six Degrees of Separation**, **Oleanna** and **My Night With Reg**. But without public subsidy it would close immediately and its unique place in British theatre would be lost. If you care about the future of arts in this country, please write to your MP and say so.

Stage Hands Appeal

Royal Court Theatre

A MODEL THEATRE

You've seen the show, read the playtext and eaten the ice-cream - but what to do with all the loose change left over from the evening's entertainment? The Royal Court's 'Model Money Box' may be just the answer. The money box is a replica model of the new-look Royal Court, complete with undercroft cafe, new circle bar balcony and re-shaped auditorium. Notes and coins will be gratefully received.

Many thanks to everyone who has supported the Stage Hands appeal so far. Our goal, to raise over £500,000 from friends and audience members towards the £16 million redevelopment of the Royal Court Theatre, Sloane Square, has already raised £160,000 - a great start.

A special thank you to everyone who is supporting us with covenanted donations: covenants are particularly important because we can claim back the tax a donor has already paid, which increases the value of the donation by *over one third* (at no extra cost to the donor). The same applies to Gift Aid, which adds one third to the value of all single donations of £250 or more. It is vital we make the most of all our donations so if you're able to make a covenanted contribution to the theatre's Stage Hands Appeal please call 0171-930 4253.

BUILDING UPDATE

Both our Lottery grant and partnership funding are hard at work for us now as the Redevelopment in Sloane Square continues apace. With the stripping out-process almost complete, and the stage, seats, fixtures and fittings all removed, we can start to get down to the project's three 'Rs'; Re-structuring, Re-building and Refurbishing.

Hoardings will shortly be going up around the front of the theatre, securing the site and providing building access, which means that the much-loved Royal Court Theatre facade will disappear from view for a while. However, out-of-sight (or should that be site?) is definitely not out-of-mind and a photo display in the Theatre Downstairs lobby will provide building updates as the work progresses.

Stage Hands Appeal

40TH ANNIVERSARY GALA

The Porchester Hall in Queensway, once notorious for its drag balls and Turkish baths, was the venue for the Royal Court's recent 40th Anniversary gala, hosted by The New Yorker and Hugo Boss.

The centrepiece of this glittering evening was a cabaret directed by the Court's Artistic Director, Stephen Daldry, and as the 450 diners laid down their silverware an explosion shook the room and thirty chefs and waitresses from Arnold Wesker's *The Kitchen* burst onto the stage. But it wasn't just the cast from *The Kitchen* and David Storey's *The Changing Room* who provided the entertainment: Jeremy Irons' rendition of a piece from Christopher Hampton's *Savages*, backed by authentic South American musicians, hushed the room; Sloane Square favourites Kens Cranham and Campbell performed a piece from *Waiting for Godot*; Harriet Walter re-created her role from Timberlake Wertenbaker's *Three Birds Alighting on a Field*, offering a hilarious portrait of the socialite finding salvation through art; and Stephen Fry delivered PG Wodehouse's wonderful poem, *The Audience at the Court Theatre*.

Famous faces including Melvyn Bragg, Nigel Hawthorne, Helen Mirren, Ruby Wax, Salman Rushdie, Mick Jagger, Jerry Hall and Vanessa Redgrave were thrilled by the theatrical magic of the evening and the money raised by the gala will play an important part in getting the redevelopment work in Sloane Square off the ground.

TAKE YOUR SEATS

There will be 400 new seats in the refurbished Theatre Downstairs and 60 in the Theatre Upstairs - all of which are offered 'for sale'. Not only will the seats in the Theatre Downstairs have the printed name of the seat's 'owner', they will also bear the owner's *signature*. Seats may be bought on behalf of children and grandchildren and can be signed by the children themselve. Companies are also eligible to take part in the scheme and their business logos will printed on the plaques.

For details of the 'Take A Seat' scheme please call 0171-930 4253.

STAGE HANDS T-SHIRTS

Stage Hands T-shirts are now on sale at the Bookshop in the Theatre Downstairs and in the bar at the Theatre Upstairs, price £10.

For futher details about Stage Hands and the

Redevelopment

please call the

Development

Office on

0171-930 4253

For the Royal Court

DIRECTION
Artistic Director
Stephen Daldry
Assistant to the Artistic Director
Marieke Spencer
Deputy Director
James Macdonald
Associate Directors
Elyse Dodgson
Ian Rickson
Garry Hynes*
Max Stafford-Clark*
Caroline Hall (Gerald Chapman Award)
Roxana Silbert*
Stephen Warbeck (music)*
Trainee Director
Rufus Norris #
Casting Director
Lisa Makin
Literary Manager
Graham Whybrow
Literary Assistant
Jean O'Hare
Literary Associate
Stephen Jeffreys*
Resident Dramatist
Martin Crimp+
International Assistant
Aurélie Mérel

PRODUCTION
Production Manager
Edwyn Wilson
Deputy Production Manager
Paul Handley
Production Development Manager
Simon Harper
Head of Lighting
Johanna Town
Senior Electricians
Alison Buchanan
Lizz Poulter
Assistant Electricians
Marion Mahon
Lars Jensen
LX Board Operator
Matthew Bullock
Head of Stage
Martin Riley
Senior Carpenters
David Skelly
Christopher Shepherd
Terry Bennet
Head of Sound
Paul Arditti
Deputy Sound
Simon King
Sound Assistant
Neil Alexander
Production Assitant
Mark Townsend
Head of Wardrobe
Jennifer Cook
Deputy Wardrobe
Neil Gillies
Sam Mealing

MANAGEMENT
Executive Director
Vikki Heywood
Assistant to the Executive Director
Susie Songhurst
Administrator
Alpha Hopkins
Finance Director
Donna Munday
Re-development Finance Officer
Neville Ayres
Finance Assistant
Rachel Harrison
Project Manager
Tony Hudson
Assistant to Project Manager
Monica McCormack
Administrative Assistant
Sarah Deacon

MARKETING & PRESS
Marketing Manager
Jess Cleverly
Press Manager
(0171-565 5055)
Anne Mayer
Marketing Co-ordinator
Lisa Popham
Publicity Assistant
Peter Collins
Box Office Manager
Neil Grutchfield
Deputy Box Office Manager
Terry Cooke
Box Office Sales Operators
Emma O'Neill
Laura Brook
Sophie Pridell
Ruth Collier*
Valli Dakshinamurthi*

DEVELOPMENT
Development Director
Joyce Hytner
Development Manager
Jacqueline Simons
Development Co-ordinator
Sue Winter*
Development Assistant
Tracey Nowell

FRONT OF HOUSE
Theatre Manager
Gary Stewart
Deputy Theatre Managers
Yvette Griffith
Tim Brunsden
Duty House Manager
Rachel Fisher
Relief Duty House Managers
Sarah Harrison
Anthony Corriette
Lorraine Selby
Bookshop Supervisors
Del Campbell*
Catherine Seymour*
Maintenance
Greg Piggot*

Lunch Bar Caterer
Andrew Forrest*
Stage Door/Reception
Jemma Davies*-
Lorraine Benloss*
Charlotte Frings*
Tyrone Lucas*
Andonis Anthony*
Tom Cockrell*
Cleaners
(Theatre Upstairs)
Maria Correia*
Mila Hamovic*
Peter Ramswell*
(Theatre Downstairs)
Avery Cleaning Services Ltd.
Firemen
Myriad Security Services
(Theatre Downstairs)
Datem Fire Safety Services
(Theatre Upstairs)

YOUNG PEOPLE'S THEATRE
Director
Dominic Tickell
Youth Drama Worker
Ollie Animashawun
Special Projects
Julie-Anne Robinson
Administrator
Aoife Mannix
Outreach Co-ordinator
Stephen Gilroy

ENGLISH STAGE COMPANY
President
Greville Poke
Vice President
Joan Plowright CBE

COUNCIL
Chairman
John Mortimer QC, CBE
Vice-Chairman
Anthony Burton

Stuart Burge
Harriet Cruickshank
Stephen Evans
Sonia Melchett
James Midgley
Richard Pulford
Gerry Robinson
Timberlake Wertenbaker
Nicholas Wright
Alan Yentob

ADVISORY COUNCIL
Diana Bliss
Tina Brown
Allan Davis
Elyse Dodgson
Robert Fox
Jocelyn Herbert
Michael Hoffman
Hanif Kureishi
Jane Rayne
Ruth Rogers
James L. Tanner

*=part-time; #=Arts Coucil of England/Calouste Gulbenkian Foundation/Esmee Fairbairn Charitable Trust; + = Arts Council Resident Dramatist

For Clara

With special thanks to Winsome Pinnock
for her invaluable assistance and advice.

Thanks also to David Lan, everyone at the Royal Court,
the Royal Court Young People's Theatre,
Prue and Bob, my Ps and Bug.

Characters

Sophie, *a black woman in her late fifties.*
Mother, *a white woman, middle-aged.*
Mina, *a white girl. Twenty.*
Adele, *Sophie's daughter. A school teacher. Twenty-seven.*
Bafana, *Sophie's son. Eighteen.*

Set

As minimal as possible.

Act One

Scene One

Sophie's *house. A small kitchen opening onto a modest living-room.* **Sophie** *is icing a cake.* **Adele** *is hanging up washing outside.*

Sophie (*calling offstage*) Round the other side so that nobody can see.

Adele Why. You scared she'll see that the natives wear underwear? (*Pause.*) Brightly coloured ones *nogal* [as well]. Not a plain pair in sight.

Sophie Aai, shut up, you. Come help here and stop your nonsense.

Adele I'm about to run late. I've got to go to a meeting.

Sophie What meeting?

Adele A street meeting. For the last week we've been trying to elect a chairperson.

Sophie Why suddenly you spring this on me now?

Adele I won't be long.

Sophie But you promised me! You know how to say such clever things.

Adele I thought you always said I talk junk.

Sophie You talk nice when you want to.

Adele Why did you invite her?

Sophie She insisted. What could I say?

Adele Try no.

Sophie I couldn't.

Adele But, Ma . . .

Sophie   Don't Ma me. I want you here all the same.

Adele   You could've made an excuse.

Sophie   Please, for my sake.

Adele (*irritated*)   OK.

Sophie   Not just OK.

Adele   I'll try.

Pause.

Sophie   Don't you want something to eat before you go? You haven't even touched your coffee.

Adele   It has maggots.

Sophie   Rubbish. No one has ever heard of maggots. Not in coffee.

Adele   There – see those white bits – on top. They floating.

Sophie   That's the Cremora.

Adele   Yes. The maggoty Cremora.

Sophie *sits and drinks the coffee.*

Sophie   When she was young, she was awful. Tried ordering me around like she was Miss Somebody or something. But I'd have none of it. I felt sorry for her.

Adele   Why?

Sophie   Her mother was strict.

Adele   You were strict with us.

Sophie   Yes. Still am. But all the same. She was a nice girl. She cried like mad when I left. Yooow. Her mother had to lock her behind the security bars to stop her running out to me. And there I was sitting on the pavement, my things boxed all around me – and Mina howling her head off – as if the demons had got her!

Adele Maybe you'll be lucky. She'll help you out and get lost or hijacked.

Sophie God forbid. Bafana should meet her in Commissioner Street. I don't want no trouble. I said he must see her as she must wear a blue T-shirt.

Adele She won't need a blue T-shirt – she'll stick out like a sore thumb.

Sophie (*chuckling*) Ag, shame!

Adele I can't see why you sorry for her. She had you twenty-four hours a day, whilst I was shunted off to . . .

Sophie You got a good education. See where it's got you.

Adele I'll be late, I better go.

Sophie You won't disappoint me?

Adele I'll try.

Sophie Promise.

Adele I can't promise. I'm over committed.

Sophie Ag, you right, this coffee is terrible. Pick up some fresh milk, will you?

Adele Sure.

Sophie And, Adele . . . I want things to be nice.

Adele OK! I said OK! I'll try! What more do you want of me!

Sophie Adele, please . . .

Adele I'll try do my best for your little spoilt brat! I'll try. So you can entertain her nicely and let her carry on like she owns the place or something and I'll 'ummm' and 'ahhh!' and 'WOW' at every squeak she makes . . .

Sophie Adele, please!

Adele   No, not Adele, please! I said I'd do it! Now
LEAVE it! I also happen to have a life. You may have
nothing better to do than spend a nice afternoon playing
host to a dumb white liberal, good for you, but I haven't
quite reached that state of degradation just yet!

Sophie (*hurt*)   If you are going to behave like this it is
better you don't come.

Adele   No, I'll come.

Sophie   I don't want favours like this from you.

Adele   I'll come.

Sophie   It's better you leave it. I'm finer off alone.

Adele   Mama, please.

Sophie   No. Always this is what I get from you. Leave it,
Adele. You too keen to help other peoples. Always you
must rush off to this meeting and the next for other
peoples but for your own mother nothing!

Adele   That's not true.

Sophie   I only asked you just this once.

Adele   And I said yes.

Pause.

I said yes. I'll come. I'll go to the meeting. I'll excuse
myself early and I'll come.

Sophie   What do you have so against me?

Adele   Nothing.

Sophie   You look down on me.

Adele   No. I respect you. I admit I was wrong.

Sophie   I don't like this business either, Adele. I'm not
sure if she's up to good. After all these years to phone me
like that. And she was funny on the phone. Funny. Such a
high funny voice. No, Adele, I don't know.

Adele We'll grin and bear it – and next time we won't repeat our mistakes.

Bafana *enters.*

Bafana *Sanibonani.* [Hello, plural]

Sophie Where's she? What's wrong with my children! He hasn't bothered to fetch her! Hasn't bothered!

Bafana She's here.

Turns to find her.

Sophie But you early! Why so early?

Bafana We not early, you told me two thirty.

Sophie That's just because you are always late! I meant it for three! Where is she?

Adele Is she waiting for us to roll out the red carpet?

Sophie *(under her breath)* Not now, Adele.

Mina Sorry, I think I must have I stepped in something . . . /

Adele Dog shit . . . /

Bafana / Scrape it on the step . . . /

Sophie *(through clenched teeth)* Shut up now, you. You hear me. Shut up! Mina?

Mina *(awkward. Holding one shoe in her hand and trying to force the other off her foot)* Hello.

Sophie Owwww, Mina! Mina!!! (**Sophie** *hugs her.*) Owww. My Mina! But you've grown!!! My Mina! So big! Owww, let me have a look at you? Owww! But you big hey? And fat! So nice and fat! So nice and tall and fat!! (*Laughs.*) Who would have thought you would have grow to be so big! Always such a tiny one! I would never have recognised you! Never ever! Not in a million years!

Mina *(hurt)* Am I that different?

Bafana You not fat.

Sophie Nooo. No. No!! Not fat! No! You've grown so beautiful!! Very, very beautiful! So beautiful. After all these years, Mina! (*Pause.*) Mina, you've met my son Rejoice, eh?

Mina Yes, we've met.

Sophie But I want you to meet properly! Formal introduced! Mina – Rejoice. Maybe you got to speak a bit already on the way, no?

Mina Yes . . . Sort of.

Sophie And Mina, Adele. This is my daughter Adele. And Adele, this is Mina! The Mina I was telling you about all these years! My Mina! And now look! So tall and grown up and beautiful and she's come back to me! My Mina!

Adele My mother often spoke about you.

Sophie Maybe you remember, Mina? Adele came over to play once or twice. Maybe you was too small. I don't know.

Mina No, no. You came swimming the one time.

Adele Yes. That's right.

Mina And Sophie tied a rope around your waist and dangled you in the water so you wouldn't drown!

Sophie Yooow! She was so scared of the water!

Adele I was not.

Sophie I was tug-tugging on the rope and she screamed so loud that I thought she was going to drown! Yoow! I remember! Adele could scream like nothing on earth as a child! (*Pause.*) But enough of this formal-formal stuff – come, let's all go and sit down. No, on the good chairs, here in the lounge. Adele can make us all tea. That is if you want tea, Mina? Anything, tea, coffee, cold drinks? We have anything you want! Anything!

Mina Whatever's easiest.

Sophie No, you must decide.

Mina I don't mind.

Sophie Choose! Choose! Whatever, Mina! Coke or Sprite or orange juice? You like orange juice?

Mina Anything.

Sophie Whatever you want, whatever!

Adele Let her have tea.

Sophie Aai, Adele. She must decide.

Mina Yes, tea'll be great, thank you.

Sophie And I've made a cake special for you. A chocolate one! Your favourite!!

Mina You shouldn't have gone to any trouble!

Sophie No trouble! No trouble is too much trouble for my Mina! (*Laughs.*) Go put the water on, Adele, for tea for poor Mina. (*Aside to* **Bafana**.) Quickly run to the spaza and get us some milk. (*To* **Mina**.) Yoow. But the milk doesn't keep nice in this weather!

Mina We can have whatever. I don't mind.

Sophie No, you just relax, Mina.

Bafana I need money.

Sophie What's happened to the twenty rands I gave you this morning?

Bafana It's finished.

Sophie Rubbish! How can it be finished?

Bafana I used it for the taxi. For both of us.

Sophie All of it? (**Bafana** *looks surly.*) OK! OK! No problem! No problem. (**Sophie** *scratches in a tin on the shelf.*) Yoow! But Rejoice can eat money, Mina! Have you noticed that, Mina? How boys know how to eat money? Like nothing on earth! (*Aside.*) Get it on credit.

Bafana *exits.*

Mina It's a nice room.

Sophie (*genuinely pleased*) You like it.

Mina Yes.

Sophie It's not so grand. Hey, not like your mother's place! But you like it?

Mina Yes!

Sophie After all these years. God led you to me! After all these years!

Mina I looked you up in the phone book.

Sophie Ja! Like I always said. God would lead my Mina to me through the phone book! I always said that! Didn't I, Adele! From the day when you cried like that when I left, I said: 'She'll look me up, my Mina! We'll be reunited yet.' That's what I said, not so, Adele?

Adele Yes.

Mina I missed you.

Sophie Yooow! And I missed you really, Mina! Nothing could replace my Mina! Even the little Van Rooyen girl who I liked so much couldn't replace my Mina!

Mina Who?

Sophie The little girl at the place two after. Christina Van Rooyen. They were wonderful to me, you know, Mina, that family. If it wasn't for my legs I would have been there forever! Mrs Van Rooyen was like a mother to me. She still sends me a Christmas box every year!

Bafana *returns. He hands the milk to* **Adele** *and leaves the room.*

Mina That's nice.

Sophie   Ja. But enough about me. Tell me about you. I want to hear everything. Everything.

Mina   There is not much to tell.

Adele *brings in the tea.*

Adele   Sugar?

Mina   No thanks.

Sophie   That's why you so thin, Mina! You take no sugars! I take seven!!

Mina   Seven?

Sophie   Ja! Seven! You don't remember? I used to give you tea with sugar and condensed milk there by my room? See! (*Putting in the sugar.*) One, two, three . . .

Adele   It's been wonderful meeting you, Mina. But unfortunately I have an urgent meeting to attend.

Sophie   Ag, leave it, Adele. If you miss one, it won't matter.

Adele   I'd love to stay, honest. But I've got to go.

Sophie   It's always meetings, meetings! She'll be the death of me with her meetings.

Adele   I'll be back as soon as possible.

Sophie   Ja, I'm sure Mina wants to talk to you.

Mina   It's all right, I understand. Maybe we can make another time.

Adele   I'll hurry.

Adele *exits.*

Sophie   Always rushing off somewhere that one! It would be nice the two of yous to talk a bit.

Mina   I'd like that.

Sophie   Ja.

Pause.

Ja, just to talk-talk a bit. Mina. Ja.

Pause.

Ja . . . so . . . I want to know everything – everything since last I saw you.

Mina   Yes.

Sophie   You must be finished now with school, Mina?

Mina   Yes.

Sophie   And you by the university?

Mina   Yes.

Sophie   Ja, I can see you clever like Bafana, eh? He said for you that he is by the university, Mina?

Pause.

Mina   Actually I don't think I'll go back. It's not that I failed or anything, it just seems so useless. I just want to get a job and earn some money . . . so that I'm not so dependent on my mother . . .

Sophie   Aai, she likes too much to fight your mother . . .

Mina   Ja. (*Pause.*) I always meant to come. (**Sophie** *nods.*) Then the other day I found this bracelet. (*Indicating her black rubber bracelet.*)

Sophie   Ja . . .

Mina   You must have given it to me to keep the *tokoloshe* [spirit] away.

Sophie   Oh.

Mina (*hurt*)   You don't remember?

Sophie   No! No! Of course. For the *tokoloshe*, of course. I must have gave it to you because you was such a nervous child. Remember, Mina? And you was such a nervous child. So nervous. Nervous. Your mother would walk out

the door and you'd start to go Nagh! Nagh! Nagh! the
whole time. I would always have to run to you – you was
too scared to even move out of the bed.

Mina (*enjoying the fact that* **Sophie** *has remembered her*)   Yes.

Sophie   And you used to pish! In the bed! Like a baby!
Pish! In the middle of the night! And I'd get you up to take
you to the toilet and then again you'd go – pish! In the
bed!

Mina   That was only when I was very young!

Sophie   Rubbish! Right up 'til you was ten, eleven,
twelve, thirteen, fourteen! Mina! You was old! And still in
the middle of the night yous was going pish in the
bed!

Mina   You left when I was about nine.

Sophie   So young?

Mina   Maybe ten. No, I was nine. I was in Standard
Three.

Sophie   Ag, but anyways you was a pisher. Even Rejoice
and Adele never pished like that! And the toilet was outside
and they slept in, in those days. Not like you. Never.

Mina   That's not true, not always.

Sophie   Always. Ja! You used to pish!

Mina   I remember once saying my prayers, long after,
when I was at university. And I never wet the bed then,
never! Really, Sophie! I promise! And I ended it off 'And
please God let me not wet the bed tonight!' As if I was still
a little kid. And I laughed out loud, because I had
forgotten that I had grown up and I didn't need to pray
for that any more!

Laughs.

Sophie   You don't pish any more, I can see that.

Mina   No.

Sophie   Ja. And I see you've become early. You used to always be late.

Mina   Still am.

Sophie   But you was early today.

Mina   I got the time wrong. I waited for Rejoice for ages.

Sophie   Yooow! You should have told me! I'm sorry! You waited! Alone?

Mina   No, it was my fault. I'm bad with time.

Sophie   Ag, shame, but you always was, neh, Mina? It's a sickness to always be late.

Mina   Yes.

Sophie   Thanks God I brought my children up to be early.

Mina   Well, you failed when it came to me.

Sophie   If you were my daughter I would have beaten it into you!

Mina   I doubt it.

Sophie   I've never been late in my life.

Mina   My mother never seemed to think that.

Sophie   *Aikhona!* [No!] Never you mind your mother. Not once. My bad legs and all. Five, six, seven o'clock – I was there. In the kitchen . . . cleaning – cleaning nice, doing breakfast, whatnot. I was there! Still Sundays I go by foot, all the way to the church in Rockville. Imagine, from here to Rockville and it's far, Mina! Deep Soweto, Mina – deep! And I'm first there. Even before they unlock the gate. I'm waiting. Never in my life late! Yoow, Not me!!! Never! Not me! So don't tell me that about your mother!

Mina   Sorry.

Pause.

Sophie   Well. Otherwise, how is your mother?

Mina   Fine. She's fine.

Pause.

Sophie   And she is still nursing at Hillbrow?

Mina   Yes.

Sophie   And she's not scared? I tell you I'm scared of Hillbrow. What with the drugs and foreigners – these *makwere-kwere* [foreigners] rubbish they's bad news, Mina. No thanks! I don't want nothing with Hillbrow!

Mina   My mother seems to think it's OK!

Sophie   She's very brave. Like you. I can see you are not scared nowadays. Not like before. You've grown up so nice!

Mina   Thank you.

Sophie   Just like your mother.

Mina   I'm not at all like my mother!

Sophie   No, not exactly like your mother. You more your father's child.

Mina   I don't think I'm like either.

Sophie   When you young, you can't tell these family things. That only comes much later.

Adele *enters. She slams the door behind her and tries to force a smile.*

Adele   You haven't cut the cake.

Sophie   Yoow! How did you creep back! We was so busy talking we never heard you!

Adele   It was cancelled.

Sophie   You care too, too much, Adele! You the only one who is always there!

Adele   Should I cut?

Sophie   Of course! Of course! I forgot. Specially for you, Mina! Chocolate! Like you always like!

Mina   How do you remember?

Adele   Everyone loves chocolate.

Sophie   Let Mina cut. And make a wish.

Adele   That's for birthdays.

Sophie   Today is like a birthday! Go on, Mina, close your eyes and wish!

Mina   OK.

Sophie   And what did you wish for?

Adele   You can't ask. It's secret.

Sophie   No, fine. Here let me cut for you, Mina.

Mina   Only a small bit.

Sophie   Rubbish, the biggest slice. It's your cake.

Mina   No. I'm not hungry.

Sophie   Aai! You must never refuse food, Mina. It is against our culture. Because if you refuse food in our culture it shows you think it is poisoned and that you don't trust us.

Mina   I know it's not poisoned.

Sophie   All the same, we must teach you our ways if you here to visit us!

Adele   Leave her – it doesn't matter.

Sophie   No, it does, Adele. We must teach her. She must learn. We must learn how it is to sit down together in this country and eat cake.

Adele   We first must learn how to redistribute the cake.

Sophie (*laughing*)   You and your meetings! (*Pause.*) So. You was saying your mother is very well eh?

Mina   Yes, yes. She's well. She's still working very hard/

Sophie   Ag, shame – but your mother is too much in love with that hospital. She will never ever want to leave that place. Not 'til the day she dies!

Mina   She is not so happy there actually. Sometimes she talks about moving to private. She thinks that the standard has gone down. She says that other nurses are lazy, and the strikes are terrible.

Adele   Which other nurses?

Mina   I don't know. The ones she works with.

Sophie   Oh . . .

Adele   The black ones?

Mina   I never said that.

Adele   But you meant it.

Mina   I did not. That's the kind of thing my mother would say, not me. (*Pause.*) Anyway, who are the people really affected by the strikes? Certainly not rich whites from Sandton.

Adele   Really?

Mina   Yes. It's poor people. Those who can't afford anything else. Ask Sophie. Who are the people affected by the strikes?

Pause.

Sophie   It is not so easy for them, Mina. They give up a lot. They receive no money and they have families to look after.

Adele   And terrible conditions. It's obvious why they are forced to strike.

Long pause. Awkward. **Mina** *coughs.*

Adele   My mother wanted me to be here because she thinks I talk nice.

Mina   Yes.

Adele   I think I'm actually a conversation killer.

Mina *laughs.*

Mina (*trying to make a joke*)   My mother says that at one of the hospitals in the intensive care unit, the patient in bed two died every Thursday. They didn't know why until they discovered that on Thursday the cleaning staff unplugged the life support machines, so they could plug in the floor cleaner.

Pause.

Adele   Did your mother say anything else?

Mina   No.

Adele   Pity. She sounds vaguely more interesting. Next time send your mother.

Sophie   Adele – I'd like to see you together with Mina's mother.

Enter **Bafana**.

Sophie   I'm telling you he's like a fly this boy. He can smell food a mile away. That's the only time you'll see him! Cut for yourself and join us.

Bafana   I've got to study.

Adele   My foot you've got to study. Come, comrade, show some solidarity.

Sophie   Aai, Adele.

Mina   It's getting late, maybe I should be going.

Sophie   You just got here!

Bafana   Ja, stay.

Sophie   My Rejoice, he's the very clever one. So young, and almost going to graduate!

Bafana   At least I'm not an old-timer, like some of those students. I'd hate that. To be so old and still studying.

Mina   Yes.

Bafana   So? What do you think of this Soweto?

Mina   It's nice. I like it.

Adele   And the poverty?

Mina   It is not that nice.

Adele   So what do we do about it?

Mina (*mumbles*)   I don't know. Socialism.

Adele   Oh, good girl. Words spoken from a Marxist text-book.

Mina   I've never read Marx.

Adele   But you still like to spout it.

Sophie   Adele!

Bafana   At least you here. Usually whites don't like coming here cos they don't want to have to face up to apartheid.

Adele   She is sightseeing.

Bafana   Whites don't even like talking about apartheid.

Mina   No, I think that's all anyone ever wants to talk about – apartheid.

Adele   Oh, so do you think everything in the world is happy? Just trees and flowers and sunshine?

Mina   No, but I think apartheid is our national obsession. We all eat, sleep, breathe, talk apartheid. Every book, every TV show, every radio programme is nattering on about apartheid. Do you think Germans spend their lives talking about the fact that they baked six million Jews in the oven?

Adele   You crass.

Mina   I'm not. I'm honest.

Adele   You are insensitive and you are racist.

Mina   I'm not.

Adele   How do you know?

Mina   Cos I'm here.

Adele   It means nothing. We are forced into a white world. You have a choice. You don't have to be here . . .

Mina   I'm not so sure.

Adele   Why?

Mina   I don't know.

Adele   Don't you have any opinions?

Uncomfortable pause.

Sophie   How is your grandmother?

Mina   Fine. She's in a home.

Sophie   Ag, shame – she never wanted that.

Mina   She was too frail. We couldn't manage with her.

Sophie   I suppose it's always like that. Sometimes I think Adele would box me away too if she could. She's just waiting to nail me into my coffin.

Adele   That's rubbish, I wouldn't.

Sophie   Nobody knows what's coming for them.

Mina   Yes, things are pretty unstable.

Adele   They are improving.

Bafana   I don't see very much happening.

Mina   I agree, just a lot of false promises.

Adele   Don't worry, we'll manage. If we could survive

forty years of apartheid then we can survive forty more years of what you like to see as false promises. We'll manage without you.

Mina   What I meant was . . .

Adele   Ag, shame, poor little girl, why don't you just banish yourself to Europe.

Mina   What did he just say? 'Things aren't happening.' How come he can say that and I can't?

Adele   You have to earn your right to criticise.

Sophie   Don't always take her too seriously. She's upset – she never got her chance to talk herself out at her meeting.

Adele   It has nothing to do with my meeting.

Mina   Well, what then?

Adele   What do you really want with us?

Mina   How do you mean?

Adele   Ten years is a long time to go searching for someone you really love.

Mina   I always wanted to.

Adele   So why didn't you.

Mina   I couldn't. I was a child.

Sophie   Ja, Adele. She was too young.

Adele   Sure.

Mina   I suppose I came . . . cos I have nothing.

Sophie   Rubbish, Mina, you have everything! Everything! Other people would die to have what you've got.

Adele   You're acting like a spoilt brat. You are ungrateful.

Mina   I'm not.

Adele   You are. It's not enough what you've got. You want to be part of what we've got too.

Sophie   Aai, but, Adele, you like to argue!

Mina   It's getting late. I think I should be going.

Sophie   Stay.

Mina   It's starting to get dark.

Sophie   All right then.

Adele   Dark and dangerous.

Mina   I'm not scared.

Adele   But you going anyway.

Sophie   Ja, you sensible, Mina. Don't listen to what she says she's full of rubbish. You must come again.

Mina   Thank you.

Bafana   I'll walk you.

Mina   Don't worry. I'm fine.

Bafana   You don't know the area. Anyway, it's our culture.

Sophie   Yoow! Mina. Walk her! You'll never find your way, Mina! Never ever in a thousand years. He must walk you.

Mina   Thank you.

Sophie *hugs* **Mina**.

Sophie   And don't leave it ten years! I want to see you soon! Not when you already married with children! You hear?

Mina   No, no, soon.

Scene Two

The street outside **Sophie**'s *house*.

Mina You really don't have to. (*Pause.*) You can walk me to the corner and then go back and pretend to your mother that you went all the way to town.

Bafana It's OK.

Mina She won't know. (*Pause.*) And don't worry, I'll manage.

Bafana It's OK. Relax.

Mina I shouldn't have come.

Bafana My mother appreciated it.

Mina Oh? Well, Adele doesn't like me.

Awkward pause.

Bafana Adele never liked you.

Mina Why?

Bafana I don't know. (*Pause.*) Maybe she was jealous.

Mina I thought you should be the one to be jealous. I was always around when you were a child.

Bafana I never noticed.

Mina Oh. (*Pause.*) Well, I certainly remember you. Sophie was always changing your nappies and stabbing you with safety pins . . . you used to stink.

Bafana Great.

Mina But you've improved with age.

Bafana How old were you?

Mina I don't know. Maybe about three.

Bafana So you what now?

Mina It's rude to ask a woman her age.

Bafana *laughs.*

Mina   I didn't mind you too much. You stank but I used to like playing with you. I always wanted a brother.

Bafana   Ja. It's nice to come from a big family. You always have someone to fight with.

Mina   I even shared your breast milk. Your mother squeezed it out for me into a jam jar. So I could taste it.

Bafana   Do you remember what it tasted like?

Mina   Like nothing. I think I threw most of it out.

Bafana   Oh.

Mina   I just wanted to taste it. Not drink the whole thing.

Bafana   Sure.

Pause.

Mina   Do you like university?

Bafana   It's boring. Predictable.

Mina   You must be clever.

Bafana (*fake modesty*)   I'm OK.

Mina   I've never seen you there.

Bafana   Well, I'm there. In any case how would you know. Before today, you've never really met me.

Mina   True.

Bafana   Maybe now we'll bump into each other more often.

Mina   Maybe.

Bafana   Ja, maybe. I could show you some interesting areas. If we walk to the top of that ridge you could look down and see Mandela's Orlando house.

Mina   Oh.

Bafana   Do you want me to take you?

Mina   . . .

Bafana   He doesn't live there any more anyway. All the politicians have now moved to the suburbs.

Mina   Yes.

Bafana   They living among whites. Just now they will forget who voted for them. They'll forget who they are. Like these stupid kids you see around here who go to private schools.

Mina   Did you go to a private school?

Bafana   Why?

Mina   I was just wondering from the way you talk.

Bafana   (*defensive*)   Well, I didn't.

Mina   OK.

Pause.

Bafana   But I'll tell you this much. I'd never do that to my children.

Mina   What?

Bafana   Send them to private schools. They'll go to school right here, in the location. They must know where they belong. Private schools are shit.

Mina   How would you know? I thought you never went.

Bafana   Well, sort of. But only for a year. For matric – so it doesn't really count. I'm not like these other private school coconut-kids, strutting around here. Specially the girls. They think they too good for anyone so they won't go out with men from the location.

Mina   Your mother wanted the best for you.

Bafana   All the other boys in my class were white. They never came to visit. Not once. They were too scared. Not like you. You different. You'd go anywhere.

Mina *laughs, embarrassed.*

Bafana   Will you come back?

Mina   Do you want me to?

Bafana *shrugs – he is non-committal.*

Bafana   Maybe. I don't know.

Scene Three

Mother'*s house. Shoes are lined up in a neat row in the entrance.*
Mother *is down on her knees scrubbing the floor.*

Mother (*warmly*)   Well, hello. Look what the cat's dragged in!

Mina   Hello.

Mother   Hey, take those shoes off.

Mina   I wiped them.

Mother   Can't you see I'm doing the floor?

Mina   They clean.

Mother   If you did a bit of work around here you'd think otherwise.

Mina   Oh for God's sake! (*Pause.*) In other houses people don't tiptoe about in socks all the time whilst we always treading on holy ground. (*She wriggles her feet out of her shoes and leaves them in a shoe rack by the door.*)

Mother   I like a clean house.

Mina   It doesn't happen in other people's.

Mother   You wouldn't last a day anywhere else. You'd drown in your own rubbish. (*Pause.*) If you've had a bad day you don't have to take it out on me.

Mina . . .

Mother I'm not your punch bag . . .

Mina There was nothing wrong with my day.

Mother No?

Mina No.

Mother I tidied your room for you. I never touched anything of yours – so you don't have to start shouting at me. I left everything where it was. Just sort of tidied around the mess.

Mina You didn't have to.

Mother What do you mean I didn't have to? I don't want things to start crawling out the entrance of that place into the rest of my house – no thank you. Even if I sprayed your whole room it wouldn't stop things . . . creeping out of there.

Mina Have you been spraying again?

Mother I have to spray.

Mina I'll kill you if you sprayed my bed.

Mother Sprayed around the bed. I just changed the sheets.

Mina Thank you.

Mother There is some chicken in the fridge. Help yourself, but mind you wipe up afterwards.

Mina I'm not hungry.

Mother All right. But once I've done the kitchen that's it. No more eating. You hear me.

Mina Yes.

Mother Well, do you have any news?

Mina No.

Mother   Well, where've you been?

Mina   Nowhere.

Mother (*humouring* **Mina**)   Ooh. Secret. Secret!

Mina   Exactly.

Mother   Don't bother. You never tell me anything anyway.

Mina   I don't have to.

Mina *goes and sits down.*

Mother   Exactly. (*Pause.*) I won't expect a decent word out of you. Next time you leave your books on the table – I'll chuck them out the window. And the washing is in the basket on your bed. Put it away. It's the least you can do.

Mina   I'll do it later.

Mother   I've heard that one before. Later means I've got to do it. Everything later! Not later, now!

Mina   Please. I'm tired!

Mother   I'm also tired.

Mina   I'll do it tomorrow. Promise.

Mother   And tomorrow you'll have some other excuse.

Mina   I've just got in. I've been running around all bloody day and I just happen to also be human and I just want five bloody minutes to relax, OK?

Pause.

Mother   What do you think? I'm the servant around here? That's what you want – someone to follow you around and wipe your arse. No, I'm not that to you, my girl. All I ask is for you to put a bit of washing away and even that is too much for her highness!

Mina   Can't I sit down for one minute without you whingeing at me about washing? Stop it and look at me.

Pause. **Mother** *just keeps cleaning.*

We must live in the most sterile place on earth. Can't you just stop for one bloody minute and talk to me?

Mother   Do you really think I enjoy cleaning? Do you really think I'm enjoying myself, Mina? That I'm having a lovely, lovely time?

Mina   Yes, as a matter of fact I do. Even when I was a child you were too busy scrubbing to cook us meals.

Mother   You hardly starved. (*Pause.*) Why don't you have a peek in the mirror. Bit on the podgy side if you ask me. Even as a child you used to look like a pregnant fairy! (*Laughs.*)

Mina   Sophie cooked for us. You were always at work.

Mother   Who?

Mina   Sophie. Even if you didn't care. At least she did.

Mother   What's suddenly with this Sophie business?

Mina   Nothing.

Mother   Sophie. Sophie Mophie. She cared about the bottle, that's all. One minute the bottle – the next the church. If it wasn't the one devil it was the other. And I came home to a filthy house – so much she cared. (*Laughs.*) Even when you ran away from home – so much she cared that she hadn't even noticed that you were gone until I got back! You were trying to walk to me at the hospital. That's how good she was to you!

Mina   I was not. I only told you that to make you feel better – because you were crying when you found me.

Mother   And you said 'Mommy – you must really love me.' That's what you said.

Mina   I was embarrassed. That's all. Standing in the middle of some strange woman's lounge and you were wallowing in tears.

Mother I was so relieved. To have my little Mina back.

Mina You were just thinking of yourself, how you would look to them.

Mother Ja, you right. I was just thinking of myself. I should have just left you there and told that woman when she phoned to put an ad in the classifieds to dispose of you like a stray dog! (*Pats* **Mina** *on the head.*)

Mina Stop it! You'll get bleach in my hair.

Mother You used to want to be blonde.

Mina I won't go blonde. I'll just get bleach marks.

Mother (*laughing*) It'd make you brush it a bit more often.

Mina It just unbrushes itself.

Mother (*she tousles* **Mina**'*s hair.* **Mina** *shifts away from her*) You've got such beautiful hair. If I had your hair − I'd brush it all right. You just don't appreciate it. Go on. Go give it a brush.

Mina I will.

Mother When? Just like your father. A procrastinator. Whenever I needed him to do anything for me around the house − he always pretended he needed the toilet. The minute he heard a dish rattle the sod headed for the loo.

Mina (*joking*) Sophie used to laugh at me and say I was vain. Cos you were always sending me off − flicking and brushing my hair.

Mother Ag, what would she know.

Mina She was a better mother to me than you could ever have been.

Mother Good. Then go live with her. See how much she likes picking up after you! And paying your bills and taking your crap. Go.

Mina I went.

Mother Oh.

Mina I did.

Mother Good for you!

Mina I mean it. This afternoon. I went to see her. At her house. It was nice.

Mother I bet. Half my stuff walked when she left. I'm sure very nice. She had long fingers that one.

Mina At least she bothered to stop and talk to me.

Mother Oh.

Mina Yes. She was pleased to see me. We all sat around talking. Me and her – and her daughter.

Mother Good communist you are. I do all the work whilst you have all the fun.

Mina That's not the point.

Mother Well, what did she want?

Mina I contacted her.

Mother (*hurt*) It's your life – do what you like.

Mina I will.

Mother Just don't expect me to get involved in it.

Pause.

And don't think you're taking my car there.

Mina You just jealous. You are such a dog in the manger.

Mother Go on. Get yourself killed.

Mina People liked me. They could see I wasn't a racist like you, that I'm different!

Mother My foot different! And do you think an AK47 bullet knows that you different? Go on, drive from one bit of kaffir country to the next. See if I care. It's your life –

do what you like with it. But don't come crawling to me
for help.

Mina   I wouldn't want it.

Mother   And put away the bloody washing. I'm not
doing everything whilst you run around doing your charity
work.

Mina   It's not . . .

Mother   Go fuck with your kaffirs – that is what you've
been wanting to do all along – off you go . . .

Mina   For goodness sake, Ma! I've done nothing. I just
visited her!

Mother   What's happened to all your old friends? To
Katherine and . . . the other one . . . Deborah. Last year
you couldn't get enough of Deborah. Now suddenly you at
university they not good enough for you and you must run
around with kaffirs.

Mina   They bore me. They've all turned into typists.

Mother   You were such a clever little girl.

Mina   So what happened?

Mother   You just don't apply yourself.

Mina   I do. I try. I really do try.

Mother   Well, try harder.

Mina   No. I just don't understand. (*Pause.*) I feel like
I'm floating in a fish-bowl. Everyone is mouthing words
at me – and I'm trapped. I don't understand.

Mother   Of course you do.

Mina   It's true.

Mother   Oh, believe what you like, we're not going
through this again.

Mina   But . . .

Mother   I'm not interested.

Mina   That's nice!

Mother   You just lazy that's all. You've had it too easy.
Spend your days with kaffirs. And believe what you like.

Mina   I just visited her.

Mother   I honestly couldn't give a damn. Just make sure
you put the washing away.

Scene Four

Sophie's *house. The setting is the same as in the first scene. Only
it is untidier.* **Adele** *sits at the kitchen table ironing a dress and
smart trousers for* **Bafana**. *He is polishing shoes and pretending
to ignore* **Mina**, *although he continuously glances up at her.* **Mina**
sits awkwardly on the edge of a chair.

Mina   Was it sudden?

Adele   He was shot.

Mina   That's awful. What happened?

Adele   He was standing in a taxi queue. The usual –
drive-by shootings.

Mina   I'm really sorry.

Adele   I've got to go over later to help as well.

Mina   Can I do anything?

Adele   No. (*Pause.*) But, thank you.

Mina   Please, if there is anything . . .

Adele   It's all right. Thanks. She said she might come
back for an hour or so – but usually with these things there

is a lot of work – so I wouldn't bank on it. I don't think there is any point in you staying.

Mina   I'm sorry about last time. You seemed upset with me.

Adele   It's OK.

Mina   No, really. Sometimes I say things which I don't really mean. I didn't want to offend you or anything.

Adele   I'm not porcelain, I won't break. Are you sure you don't want anything to drink?

Mina   I'm fine. Thanks.

Pause.

No, actually tea would be nice.

Adele   Sure.

Mina   Especially if I'm going to wait for your mother for a few more minutes. I'd like to give her my condolences. (*Following* **Adele**.) I really am sorry about your uncle.

Adele   He wasn't a real uncle. Just a man who was a very good friend to us. So we call him that.

Mina   Oh.

Bafana (*looking up from the paper. It appears as if he has been listening all the time*)   He was shot right there in Commissioner Street.

Mina   Oh.

Bafana   It was just slightly further down from where I met you that time. Where that man was – selling watches. The one who kept on asking you to marry him.

Mina   He was driving me mad.

Bafana (*imitating*)   'One day, Sissy. One day. You'll be in my hands! Just wait . . . One day, Sissy!'

Adele   Ag – *voetsak* [get out] you! (*To* **Mina**.) Next time just tell him you married. It's the only way to deal with the amorous advances of the *tsotsis* [young thugs].

Bafana Ja, he was shot right there! We certainly lead an interesting life in this country. (*Pause. Recapturing the mood.*) Not like in other countries where they lead such dull lives all they have to talk about is sex. Here at least we have hijackings and shootings and murders to amuse us! Imagine. When it's over our children will grow up to be these boring citizens who've never attended so much as a protest march! And we'll have to tell them about the good old days! 'Ja! When I was young . . . '

Mina I don't think it is that funny.

Adele Yes. I've realised. You're humourless. We have to flash a 'LAUGH NOW' sign at you every time we make a joke.

Mina I just don't like it when you trivialise issues.

Adele Trivialise issues? Oh excuse me! I see you are one of those deeeeeeeeep and sensitive people who really FEEEEL things for everyone all the time, aren't you, Mina?

Mina No.

Adele Why don't you just go off and become a social worker?

Bafana You starting again . . .

Adele Well, she's flashing her little honorary member of the holier-than-thou society badge . . . /

Mina That's not true . . . /

Adele And now on top of it all she's probably going to announce that she's a vegetarian!

Mina I'm not . . .

Adele One of those sanctimonious misunderstood – the world is so cruel and heartless leather-shoe-wearing all-innocent vegetarians!

Mina (*forceful*) I'm NOT a vegetarian.

Adele Oh. Pity. I am. I thought at least we may have one thing in common.

Pause.

Mina You really do hate me, don't you?

Adele No.

Mina Then why are you doing this to me? I'm trying to be nice!

Adele Look, I've had this all my life. I'm tired of it. It might be new and exciting and fun for you – but for me it is the old story being rehashed all over again.

Mina You were the one's making stupid jokes out of it all.

Adele (*ironic*) And you are the spoilt kid playing at revolution.

Mina The revolution is over.

Adele No. That's the problem. The revolution never happened. Just a plastic one. Our very own plastic revolution. But don't worry, it's coming. And then I don't know how safe it will be for fools like you to run around playing at it any more.

Pause.

You bring out the worst in me – you know that?

Bafana I doubt my mother is coming. She's probably very busy.

Mina Oh.

Bafana At our funerals we always prepare food for everyone to eat afterwards. It is not like with white funerals, the whole street comes! Everyone shares things.

Mina I like that.

Adele   Yes.

Bafana   Maybe you should come. My mother would like that.

Mina   No. I don't think so.

Bafana   Why? Nothing will happen. It's just an ordinary funeral.

Mina   I'll stand out. I'll be out of place.

Adele   You keep pretending that you want to be one of us – to be the same as everyone else. And then when he invites you – you say that you are not sure, that you don't know if you want to come.

Bafana   Nothing will happen to you. If he had been a gangster or something important people would be riding their cars all over the place – firing off volleys of gunshots – or maybe even burning the cars and tyres! One day I'll show you one of the exciting ones!

Mina   Yes, but I want to be a support. Not to be some out-of-place misfit.

Adele   So then be that. Just come.

Scene Five

Bafana's *room at his residence. Slow smoke-laden atmosphere.*

Bafana   If you hold a chicken's head to the ground and draw a line from its beak straight in the sand – it gets bewitched and it stays like that.

Mina   Like hell.

Bafana   It does. You just have to draw a line – like this. (*He runs his finger down* **Mina**'s *nose and along the bed.*) And it gets stuck. You have to kick it or give it a fright, otherwise it would stay like that forever.

Pause.

Mina   Sure.

Bafana   Ja, forever and ever.

Mina   . . . Or until you chopped its head off.

Bafana   Yes . . . Until you chop its head off. (*Pause.*)
When I was a child, this man bewitched me also. You
might have seen him, he was there at the funeral. He hated
my father so to get his revenge he drew a line from my
nose and I went totally mad. (**Mina** *laughs.*) I was just
standing in the yard and suddenly I saw this wave of water
crashing out of the sky engulfing me.

Mina   Rubbish. You were just thinking of the sea.

Bafana   I couldn't have been. I've never seen the sea.

Mina   You only know eternity once you've seen the sea.

Pause.

Bafana   You're strange, you know that?

Mina   It's true. Imagine all that water.

Bafana   My mother realised I had been bewitched so she
took me to an *inyanga* [traditional healer] to cure me.

Mina   And he did?

Bafana   Yes. But I still can't swim.

Mina   Good. You'll drown.

Bafana   No. (*Laughs.*) I just won't get in.

Mina   I'll push you. I'll feed you pebbles for a week and
tie a gag over your mouth so you can't spit them out – and
then I'll just hurl you off the edge into the sea.

Bafana   You've been watching too many movies.

Mina   Probably. Or I'd just leave you there. And you'll
just walk into the sea and drown yourself. (*Pause.*) Only we
live in Jo'burg and the beach is too far away.

Bafana   You're crazy, you know that.

Mina   I thought you were the mad one.

Bafana   Only when I was a child.

Mina   You used to hallucinate. You said you drowned.

Bafana   I never said that, you did. I said I saw water.

Mina   And all that was left were white wisps of foam.

She blows smoke in his face. Long pause.

Bafana   Adele went out with this man once.

Mina   And?

Bafana   He bewitched her. She couldn't move for a week after he left her. He used to phone her from Cape Town every day. She was all set to move there to live with him until she discovered that he had a wife.

Mina   Oh.

Bafana   He came up here to visit her and they went shopping together – for lamps. For his wife's new house.

Pause.

Mina   If I marry a millionaire will you also come shopping with me for new lamps, and then live in a hut at the bottom of my garden?

Bafana   No. I'm going to be the millionaire.

Mina   OK. So you'll still come shopping with me for lamps?

Bafana   Yes.

Mina   For just me? Or for your harem of wives?

Bafana   For you. (*Pause.*) I won't be able to afford to have a harem of wives.

Mina   Of course you could. You'd be a millionaire.

Bafana   Ja, but not that type of millionaire.

Mina   Then what *type*?

Bafana   Like now. Just a boring individual.

Mina   With no girlfriends . . .

Pause.

Bafana   Yes.

Mina *laughs.*

Bafana   I'm telling you I'm boring. When I was at my school I used to help coach the other boys in my area for the exams. Because their schools were so useless. We would pretend we were going out to study and do an all-nighter in the classroom. Then we would study 'til twelve and then go out looking for night vigils. We'd pretend we were going to give our support. But really we went for two reasons. One for the cookies and ginger beer. And two for the girls who we would pick up and take back to the classrooms.

Mina   Which girls?

Bafana   Girls from their school, in their class. Maybe girls who had gone to the vigil to sing in the choir and give their support. I don't know. Just girls. The other boys would sleep with them. But not me. I wasn't that successful. I was just boring.

Mina   That's good.

Bafana   It's not good. (*Pause.*) It's nothing. Anyway, it doesn't matter. It's the past.

Mina   Yes. (*Pause.*) And at your own school? What about the girls at your own school?

Bafana   What about them?

Mina   I don't know. What about them?

Bafana (*laughs*)   What would I need them for? It's not like I didn't have girls back in my own area. Anyway, they were all ugly.

Mina   All of them?

Bafana   Ja. They looked like boiled potatoes.

Mina *laughs.*

Bafana   Once, with my school we went away on a trip. We stayed in a hotel. The other boys sent a woman up to my room. She was Coloured, she must have worked in the hotel. She stood there telling me that she loved me and laughing. (*Pause.*) I knew they had sent her. That they were waiting downstairs so they could laugh at me. If they thought I needed someone why didn't they send me one of their own?

Mina   Is that what you wanted?

Bafana   No. If she had come of her own accord it would have been different.

Pause. **Mina** *reaches out and softly touches him.*

Mina   Here. Let me look into your eyes. I want to see your soul.

Bafana   Stop that. You loose.

Mina   How do you know?

Bafana   Everyone says that.

Mina   Oh.

Bafana   Yes.

Mina   Who's 'everyone'?

Bafana   I don't know. My friends. Everyone today at the funeral. They were warning me about you. You have no business with us. You can't even understand the language. How can you just sit with them for hours and hours listening to something you don't even understand?

Mina   Can you name one man I've slept with? One?

Bafana   I don't know. Probably lots.

Mina   Name them. Who are these hordes and masses of men who pass through my legs as if I were some kind of a construction factory? Who? Name them.

Bafana   There is something seriously wrong with you. You are not normal. You have to get over this Black thing.

Mina   Stop it.

Bafana   Why? Are you scared?

Mina   Yes.

Long pause.

Bafana (*mocking*)   You scared I'll rape you?

Mina   You wouldn't. You are too much of a coward.

Long pause.

Bafana   I don't really care about what the others say. It's none of their business. (*Pause.*) It's all right. I'm sorry. OK? Here, relax. I'll sing to you.

He strokes her hair.

Ngiyeke umfazi wami umuhle[1]
Ngiyeke abantwana bami abahle
Ngiye ku mfazi wo mlungu
Capela umfazi wo mlungu
Ungitijele uguthi ngicapele umfasi wo mlungu.

[I left my beautiful wife
I left my beautiful children
For the western woman
Beware of the western woman.
That's what he said. Beware of the western woman.]

Mina   I like that.

Bafana   Yes. It is a love song.

Mina   Oh.

---

[1] Based on a popular song by Chico Twala & Shirinda

Bafana It is about a man who leaves his wife. But it is OK – because he really loves the other woman.

Mina Oh.

Bafana Here, put your hand on my heart. Relax.

Mina I like being with you. I stop feeling so meaningless.

Bafana Ummm.

Mina And the words. What does it mean?

Bafana I'll teach you.

Act Two

Scene One

*The yard outside **Sophie**'s house. **Sophie** and **Mina** eat watermelon.*

Sophie I like to draw birds. I used to draw them for you when you was little. I hoped someday someone might see them and buy my work.

Mina And now?

Sophie Now I'm too old. I just draw them.

Mina They were nice.

Sophie You like them? Yes?

Mina Yes.

Sophie You silly to leave university, Mina.

Mina One day I'll go back.

Sophie Still, it is better whilst you are young. You can't teach an old dog nothing.

Mina No.

Sophie I want to die out here in this little piece of yard. With the sun shining right here like this.

Mina Not yet.

Sophie All the same – you've got to make plans.

Mina But it might not happen that way.

Sophie True. But I like to think it will all the same. A nice peaceful way to go. Here in my yard. With just you and me – eating watermelon! Ja! Just the two of us! No Adele and Bafana *klapping* [talking] my head off! This and that and the next thing! Just the two of us.

Mina Does Bafana come home still?

Sophie   I haven't seen him in over two weeks.

Mina   Oh.

Sophie   Which is good. Because it means he is studying. The less I see him – the harder I know he is working.

Mina   I'd like to be like Adele and teach.

Sophie   You have to go to school for that.

Mina   We should go inside. It's hot.

Sophie   Ag, just move into the shade. And spit the pips out, don't swallow. You don't want a melon to grow inside you.

Mina   It's just roughage.

Sophie   Nevertheless – you could swell up big and fat! What happens if it is twin watermelons! Or a whole bush!!!

Mina   It can't happen.

Sophie   I know plenty women who've walked around with watermelons inside them!! Lots of them . . .

Mina   You've always told me that!

Sophie   I don't know why you like so much to eat pips!

Mina   Suppose I was to be really pregnant?

Sophie   What?

Mina   Well, just suppose. Or if it was Adele or anyone. What would you do?

Sophie   Why are you asking me this?

Mina   Just suppose.

Sophie   Well, it depends with what. With watermelons! Well then I'd laugh! And if it was you I'd laugh even harder! I'd wait 'til the bush came creeping out of your mouth – and then I'd secure it to the ground – and you'd stand all day next to my wall – with my watermelon plant growing out of your mouth. And I'd warn all the children

in the street that this is what happens to you if you eat
pips! And they'll laugh! I'll have to tell people that although
she might look strange to them – to me she is still my little
watermelon plant after all!

Mina   And if it was not a joke? If it was real and not
watermelons?

Sophie   What are you trying to say?

Pause.

Mina   I don't know. Maybe . . .

Sophie   What?

Mina   Nothing.

Sophie   You pregnant, eh?

Mina   No! What makes you say that?

Sophie   I can tell, all right.

Mina   Well, you wrong.

Sophie   No, Mina, I may be getting on in years – but
I can smell a rat chewing away at the cheese in its trap.

Mina   I'm just asking . . .

Sophie   What will your mother say?

Mina (*admitting*)   I can't tell her.

Sophie (*flattered*)   So you come to me.

Mina   I suppose.

Pause.

Sophie   Ja, I'm a mother to you.

Mina   Yes.

Sophie   There is nothing for you to do – but find the
father – and you force him to marry you. And if he won't,
you send him here and I'll *donder* [hit] him for you. He'll
crawl away here so battered even the ants won't eat him!
He'll marry you all right!

Mina   And if he's found someone else?

Sophie   Ag, that is the way with men. You have to force them. And if after all that he refuses – at least you can get him to pay for the child. You must write down the dates of your last period and make sure you tell him that you've slept with no other man since. For your sake I hope you know whose it is. If not, I feel sorry for you.

Mina   I know for sure whose it is.

Sophie   For sure?

Mina   Yes. For sure. It just happened. I didn't mean it to.

Sophie   Of course it is never meant – this business. You go and talk to him. And you come back here and tell me. I'll help you. As much as I can.

Mina   Thank you.

Pause.

Sophie   A man from your work, was it?

Mina   Ummm.

Sophie   They won't be happy when they hear after only three weeks and you ready to leave them. What with jobs so difficult to find – and you with no proper education.

Mina   Maybe I can stay.

Sophie   Maybe. But if truth be told they'll be waiting to kick you out! Nobody wants a pregnant woman on their staff.

Mina   Things are changing.

Sophie   For us, Mina – things never change.

Mina   Are you disappointed in me?

Sophie   (*thinks*)   I expected better.

Mina   I'm sorry.

Sophie   It doesn't matter.

Mina   Maybe I shouldn't have said anything . . .

Sophie   No. I'm glad you spoke. In any case – you can't
hide a child forever – it would speak up for itself. (*Pause.*)
If you was Adele! I'd kill you. But I'll leave that for your
own mother to do.

Mina   I'm really sorry.

Sophie   You must tell that to God. Not me. It's for Him
to forgive. If you were my daughter I'd call you up in front
of all the church and make you repent your sin. (*Pause.*) Ag,
but maybe He understands that it's not just you. It's also
them. With all their rubbish talk. That they love you. They
tell that to everyone. I've seen them. One minute telling
one girl that they love her, and twenty minutes later it is a
new woman – they walking there in the street. And you
want to hit him or her for believing in it. But then you
remember what it is like to be young, so you just feel sorry.

Mina   I can feel it growing.

Sophie   How long is it?

Mina   A few weeks – that's all.

Sophie   Then – you can feel nothing yet!

Pause.

Mina   . . .

Sophie   If it is a girl you can call it after me. And bring
her to visit and we'll sit here all three of us in the sun.

Mina   And eat watermelon?

Sophie   No. You'll feed her milk and we'll eat the watermelon. Anyway – after so much watermelon – she'll be sick
of watermelon! She'll grow up hating watermelon and she'll
tell her own children one day that it is because her mother
eat so much of it whilst she was pregnant. In fact her
mother at first thought she was a watermelon!!! (*She laughs.*)

Mina   I'm not going to have it.

Sophie What d'you mean?

Mina I'll have an abortion. (*Pause.*) I will. I really will.
I hate it! Every bit of it! It's a worm! It's ruining my life!

Sophie No.

Mina Yes! I hate it! I do! It is eating this pink goo and
growing. I wish I could starve it. It's like having worms.
Like this big fat tapeworm which is eating all my food and
living off my body.

Sophie It's not the child's fault. Think of it as that little
girl – eating melon with us here in the sun.

Mina It belongs in somebody else.

Sophie Rubbish – that's the one thing you can be sure
of. As a woman it is all yours.

Mina I shouldn't have told you! I should have just done it!

Sophie You had to tell someone. In any case I would
have smelt you out.

Mina I don't care.

Sophie Well, I do! You are not running off after more
nonsense! I'll tell your mother.

Mina Do what you like.

Sophie There would be none of us left in the world if
every time a woman had a child she killed it.

Mina Other women can have them!

Sophie Then that's what you must do. Have the child
and give it to another woman to bring up for you.

Mina No! I'll lose my job!

Sophie You'll find another one!

Mina I'm stupid!

Sophie You not stupid. Look at me! I haven't a Standard
Four and I've worked all my life.

Mina   As a servant!

Sophie (*hurt and angered*)   And what's wrong with that?

Mina   Nothing.

Sophie   But for me, hey? You think you are too good for it, eh?

Mina   No.

Sophie   You with your rubbish education! Everyone these days has matric! All over in the townships they passing! And well! And you still thinking because you are white everything must come to you easy!

Mina   I can't have it!

Sophie   I thought you were cleverer than that! And look at you! Your worm! Not even a child – a worm! If you have it – it's one thing – but if you kill it – it's a different story. I want nothing to do with a woman who can kill a child.

Mina   It's Bafana's.

Sophie   What?

Mina   The child.

Sophie   My Bafana? (**Mina** *nods.*) You and Bafana? What? Since when? Don't give me that nonsense!

Mina   It's true.

Sophie   How do you know that?

Mina   It must be.

Sophie   Since when?

Mina   I didn't mean it.

Sophie   Here, under my own roof!

Mina   No! Not under your roof!

Sophie   Ag, *tula wena!* [shut up] What difference where!

Look what you've done to me – I open my house to you and this is what you go trap my son into! I'll kill you! And him! Both of you!

Mina I didn't mean it!

Sophie You didn't mean it! And who else is there then? How do you know it is him? Here you come into our lives ruining my son's chances!

Mina I'm sorry!

Sophie Rubbish you sorry! Look what you've done to me – after everything!

Mina It was him too.

Sophie Ja! But you make the choices. All men are weak! If you were a good girl you would never have been here in the first place.

Mina No. It wasn't like that!

Sophie Get out! Look what happens – I ask you into my house and you bring me nothing but disaster! I knew! I knew from the start and I'm telling you! And Adele – she could smell it too! And I said! That girl is up to no good! I don't want her near me! I said! But then I had pity for you! Stupid ha? Stupid!! And I let you come over! And now. Look! Like letting a snake in through the front door! Look what you've done to my life! GO! Mina! And do what you like. Kill your baby! Eh! Look at you – your tapeworm! Not even a baby! *Wat* ever!! A bloody tapeworm she calls it! GO!

Mina Go where?

Sophie To your mother. Anywhere. You don't belong here.

Mina I can't.

Sophie Then starve on the streets! I care nothing!

Mina I'm sorry!

Sophie From the moment you phoned I knew you were trouble and I was right!

Mina I'm sorry.

Sophie It's too late. Too, tooo late.

Mina You said you'd help me!

Sophie Ja! But then you betrayed me! I can't do nothing for filth!

Mina Please . . .

Sophie Please what?

Mina I've got nothing!

Sophie And so? You want to leave me with nothing also? Off you go! Run off to all your men here in the location, black ones, white ones, whatever, everywhere! Go and stand on the corners in Hillbrow – it's where you belong!

Mina Don't scream at me.

Sophie I've got to scream, all right! The lot of you! Hear nothing unless I scream! I look forward to being in my grave! The only one I don't have to scream at is God and even He is deaf sometimes!

Mina Sophie, please!

Sophie Don't Sophie me! I am Mrs Kunene to you!

Mina Sorry.

Sophie God will strike you down for this! Trapping my son! He's clever – at school – not like you. He's got a future. And here you are standing in my yard talking about killing the seed of my house.

Mina I didn't mean it. I didn't.

Sophie No? Then what brought you? (*She pulls the bracelet from* **Mina**'s *arm*.) Magic demons in a piece of rubber?

Mina It was supposed to protect me.

Sophie Ja! But it brought trouble.

Mina What makes you think I wanted this?

Adele (*entering*) What's wrong? I heard you both screaming all the way from down the road!

Sophie What do you expect when this . . . thing . . . is in my yard, eh?

Adele The two of you are trying to broadcast everything to the whole area? Eight o'clock News live couldn't do better!

Sophie Ja! Of course. On top of everything. She want the whole neighbourhood to know.

Mina I wasn't the one screaming.

Sophie You screamt yourself all right!

Mina Screamed.

Sophie Screamed, screamt whatever! This is Africa! And in Africa we talk African-English. Go and tell that to your Queen. Off you go. Out. Finished and *klaar* [finished].

Mina I thought you cared about me.

Sophie Well, you thought wrong. Very, very, very wrong. You were a job. That's all. And you the worst of the whole bunch *nogal*. The whole time from day one you was crying! And you was very, very rude to me always! Always trying to order me – this that and the next thing. Ja! You and your mother. She throwing her crumbs everywhere about the house to check up that I cleaned – and you too. You used to make work for me deliberate – and just before your Mother came home *nogal*. If I won't do what you say – you'd throw stuff on the floor – so that I must clean – and your mother would come home and shout for me.

Mina All kids do stupid things like that.

Sophie   Not all. You. You think you are so important to us! Well, you not! You nothing. Just one stupid girl who all the time we must always put up with.

Mina   Why do you tell me this now? Why not before. When I phoned. Why didn't you just say to me. No. You can't come. Then all this wouldn't have happened.

Sophie   I'm saying it now. Goodbye. I don't want you.

Mina   Why weren't you honest with me from the start?

Silence.

Answer me. I'm asking you a question for God's sake!

Sophie   I don't take orders. You not any more my job. I owe you nothing. (*Pause.*) We don't want you here. Me, Bafana, Adele, specially Adele. All of us. Even the floor of this house doesn't want you here!

Adele (*practical*)   Have you told him?

Mina   Who?

Adele   Bafana. Who else. I am right it's Bafana?

Sophie   From this *isibotho* [cheap woman] rubbish we can't believe nothing.

Mina   I've tried. But he won't come to the phone. In any case he's found someone else.

Sophie   Ja. So now you know. So there's nothing for you to do. On your way, go! (*Picking up a broom and sweeping at* **Mina***'s feet.*) *Voetsak! Vaai!* [get out] Out of my yard this minute.

Adele   Stop that. Let her talk.

Sophie   Talk what? She doesn't want the child. With her you can talk-talk nothing! Come, let's just go in and she can bang all she wants. We don't open the door nothing for her. Adele, come. (**Sophie** *goes in.*)

Adele   Wait.

Sophie   I'm telling you. I'm giving you three minutes.
Counting from now – and if you not on you way past hell
and gone, you don't want to know what'll happen. Adele,
come.

Bangs door. Pause.

Mina   Has he said anything to you?

Adele   Not much.

Mina   What? Did he tell you about her?

Adele   He doesn't like introducing me to his girlfriends.
He thinks he has so many that it might confuse me. I
might get their names wrong.

Pause.

Mina   He told you about me?

Pause.

Adele   Yes . . . Whatever's been happening between the
two of you . . . ?

Mina   What did he tell you?

Pause.

Adele   If you pregnant don't you think you should tell
him?

Mina   Will you phone for me?

Adele   Why? Do you think I'm your messenger?

Mina   Just ask to speak to him, if it's you he'll come to
the phone. (*Pause.*) Please, just this once, as a favour . . .

Adele   . . .

Mina   For God's sake I'm only asking you to make a
fucking phone call! It's not like I haven't tried. I keep on
phoning and phoning and I know he is there. He just
thinks that now that he's found some stupid bitch I'm no
longer good enough for him. What makes her so much

better than me? (*Pause.*) What makes some stupid bitch all done up with her hair extensions and varnished nails so much better than me?

Pause.

I keep running it all through my head, everything. Detail by detail. I need to believe that he loved me. That at least it was something special even if it was just for then. At least if it meant something it'd be OK. The whole week I've sat riveted to every news broadcast hoping to hear his name – that he's been shot, or something. Then at least it would look OK. I wouldn't be just another . . . Even when my mother talks about her patients. Sometimes I've even hoped that one of them would be him. And I keep thinking why did he have to go and find somebody else now? Why now?

Adele   It had to come eventually.

Mina   Why?

Adele   He can't help it. He's spent the last ten years at his little private school trying to be white . . . /

Mina   He was only there for matric.

Adele   That's just what he says cos he's ashamed. You came too late. He's finally got there and realised that he's actually Black. He just doesn't need you any more. (*Pause.*) Anyway. I didn't think there was anything really between the two of you in the first place.

Mina   Is that what he said?

Pause.

Adele   He wasn't planning on marrying you if that's what you want.

Mina   So it's all fine then? So now you can celebrate, hey? You and all your other moral watchdogs. You've been wanting it all along. This is just exactly what you've wanted.

Adele   I never got you pregnant.

Mina   No. But you've been trying to mess things up for me. This is what you want, hey? You're jealous.

Adele   Of what?

Mina   Of me. And your mother and him. Of everything. You can't bear the fact that she loves me too. You have a problem with her, you know that? You always caring for other people – but you do nothing for her. You always blaming her! That's what she was telling me before all this – this afternoon. About . . .

Adele   You leave my mother out of this.

Mina   Why? Cos it's true?

Adele   Isn't it enough for you that she threw you out of the house and slammed the door in your face? Do you need more? Must I do it too? We don't want you here. You stick to your own world and stay away from us.

Mina   I will.

Adele   Don't worry, we won't miss you.

Mina   Well, good, fuck you, bitch, I will! I never want to see you again! Or your mother or anything! Or him! And I'll kill this child I will! And I'll take it and throw it like shit in your faces! Because I hate you! All of you. I do! What makes you think I want to have this fucking kaffir child anyway?

Adele *slaps her. And turns to go inside.* **Mina** *grabs her.*

Mina   No, I'm sorry! I never meant it!

Adele   No, it's fine. That's what you've been like all along. Underneath. Come spit it out – admit it.

Mina   No. I never meant it. I just can't stand sticking out. And it will be worse. I walk in the street by your place and children scream after me '*Ulungu! Ulungu!*' [white] I can't take it.

Adele   People hate whites, Mina. They are taught to. From when we are very young we can see that whites are the luckiest people, they got everything. So we hate them.

Mina   Why can't we all just be normal?

Adele   It goes back. It goes back to the time when your grandfather stole my grandfather's cattle.

Mina   I just can't stand it. I want to love Africa. For my skin to blacken and for me to know that is what I am – an African. I want to be the same – like everyone else. I feel like such a foreigner. I'm a stranger. I want to go home. But then I realise I've got nowhere to go.

Adele   So stay.

Mina   How can we live with all this?

Adele   Good girl. You're growing up. Welcome to South Africa.

Sophie *opens the door.*

Sophie   Still here?

Mina   Sophie, I'm sorry.

Sophie   Well, keep your sorry. What can I do with a sorry?

Scene Two

*Outside **Bafana***'s *university residence. Late at night. It is quiet except for the occasional car and music from a party somewhere in the distance. **Bafana** has on sleeping clothes and is barefoot. His hair is unbrushed. Maybe he sleeps in one of those mass produced political T-shirts of the late eighties/nineties 'Viva Comrade Hani' style. **Bafana** is scared, he is trapped. He expresses his vulnerability by lashing out.*

Adele   Bafana! Bafana! *Vula*, man! [Open, man] *Vula! Ngiyazi ukuthi ukhona!* [I know you are there]

Bafana I'm coming. Relax! You want me to fly?

Adele You could have crawled here long ago.

Bafana *comes down. He is barefoot, in sleeping clothes, scared, awkward.*

Bafana I was sleeping.

Adele Can't we come up?

Bafana It's against the rules.

Adele And since when have you been so interested in rules?

Bafana Whose side are you on?

Adele There aren't sides.

Bafana You've joined her, eh? The two of you. Yous are plotting against me.

Adele She wants to speak to you.

Bafana (*addressing* **Mina**) Are you mad or something? Can't you phone in the morning.

Mina As if you'd answer it.

Adele Aai – you selfish, you know that! Yourself. That's all you think of!

Bafana People are watching us.

Adele I don't see any people?

Bafana By that window. At night you can't see in. They always staring out that window.

Adele So you have to dance to their tune?

Bafana I live here, not you. You want to wake the whole building?

Mina Then let us come up. It never bothered you before. (*Pause.*) Or is she in there? Is that why? Is it because of her?

Bafana Who?

Mina   Her. Your cow-eyed bitch.

Bafana   She is not a bitch.

Mina   I don't care what she is. Is it because of her?

Bafana   Yes. (*Pause. Quietly.*) It's cold. I should have put some shoes on.

Adele   You know she's pregnant.

Bafana   Yes.

Mina   How?

Bafana   Mama phoned me.

Silence.

Mina   So don't you think we should discuss it?

Bafana   There is nothing to discuss. I want nothing to do with a woman who can kill a child.

Mina   That's what you want, isn't it? That'd just suit you perfectly, hey? Well, for your information I'm going to keep my child. And don't think I'll let you even this much near it.

Bafana   Imagine that! You! Running around with a black baby on your back!

Mina   Yes, imagine it!

Adele   What's wrong with that?

Bafana   It just is.

Adele   Look. You've got to deal with it.

Bafana   . . .

Adele   Oh, so now you've gone all radical . . . and you going to pretend this is another part of your great transformation? 'Rejoice' to 'Bafana'.

Bafana   I don't have to be 'Rejoice' if I don't want to. It's a stupid name.

Adele   It was fine a few months ago when you were whiter than Mina is.

Bafana   I was never like that. She must go back to her own people. She said it herself. We are not her people. Like that time when we were driving through Eldos and she knocked a dog over. So she has to haul up this *umgodoyi* [mongrel] into the car and she's going on about how we must find the owners and get it to a vet. So I tell her that a dog is *moes* [just] a dog, and she says, 'If you people,' just like that, 'YOU PEOPLE,' 'don't know how to look after dogs, I don't know why you have them.' Those words. 'You people.' Simple.

Mina   How dare you talk about me in front of me like that!

Bafana   Shut up, you don't count. You can't understand.

Mina   I do.

Bafana   So what, you can pick up one or two things. That's all. You don't know. You so stupid you always running around singing that song I taught you and you don't even know what it means.

Mina   It's a love song.

Bafana   See? You were singing all along about what a slut you are. That I can't trust you cos you are a white bitch and a slut. And that I should never have got involved with you in the first place. Ask Adele. When I told her about it she laughed her head off with me.

Mina   You are lying.

Bafana   Ask her.

Mina (*to* **Adele**)   Is that true?

Bafana   Do you want me to translate it?

Mina (*to* **Adele**)   Is it?

Adele   Sort of.

Mina   So it means what he says?

Adele   Just leave it.

Bafana   See how stupid you are. You can't blame me for not wanting such a stupid woman to bring up my child.

Adele   It's also her child.

Bafana   Don't you join her now and start acting like a feminist.

Adele   Maybe I am a feminist.

Bafana (*pleading*)   She's trying to spoil my chances.

Mina   And me?

Bafana   It's different for you. You white. You can go back to your mother and her clean toilets.

Adele   Maybe she can't go back to her mother.

Pause.

Bafana   So what you going to do then?

Mina   I'll stay with some friends, I don't know.

Bafana   If you had any friends you wouldn't have to spend all your time with us.

Pause.

Mina   Did you never love me?

Bafana   What does it matter?

Mina   Tell me or I'll take that as a no.

Pause.

Just give me my books back.

Bafana   All of them? Even the ones I haven't read?

Mina   Yes. All of them.

Scene Three

Mother's *house. A small loft room. The sun streams in through the curtains creating a hazy orange glow.* **Mina** *is asleep. Clothes are sprawled across the room.* **Mother** *enters. She stands motionless for a few seconds.* **Mina**, *sensing her presence, awakens.*

Mother   Shhh . . . It's only me.

Mina   Oh.

Mother   It's still early, sleep.

Mina   What do you want?

Mother   Nothing.

Mina   What?

Mother   The spare towels, that's all. Sleep.

Mother *scratches through the cupboard.*

Mother   You haven't changed?

Mina   No.

Mother   You shouldn't be sleeping in one of your father's T-shirts. It's bad luck.

Mina   I had nothing else.

Mother   Here. I'll find you something. Take it off.

Mina   It's OK.

Mother   No, come change properly and get into bed. You can still sleep for an hour or so more.

Mother *passes her a nightie from the cupboard. She helps* **Mina** *into it. Kisses her on the top of her head.*

Mina   Please stay with me.

Mother   I'll be late.

Mina   Please. Just sit with me for one minute.

Mother   Tonight.

Mina One minute. I missed you.

Mother (*deflecting, laughs*) Since when do you miss me?

Mina I waited up for you. I wanted to talk to you.

Mother About what?

Mina Just wanted to talk.

Mother *goes and sits on* **Mina**'s *bed.*

Mother (*tender*) You make sure this room is cleaned up.

Mina Yes.

Mother Before I get back.

Mina Yes. (*Pause.*) I dreamt about you. I think we must have been at Galoolies Farm cos you were there with the dogs. I was hiding down by stream, but I don't know what from. I felt like I was sinking. Sucked down by the mud. I wanted to just get up and leave – but I couldn't. I was too scared to even call out to you.

Mother *rubs* **Mina**'s *arm.*

Mother It was only a dream.

Mina Yes. (*Pause.*) I'm so scared.

Mother What you scared of, my baby?

Mina I don't know. (*Pause.*) That I'll disappoint you.

Mother You go back to university and make some proper friends and you'll never disappoint me. (*Pause.*)

Mina . . .

Mother It's only another two years.

Mina (*slightly irritated*) I know.

Mother And I still have the letter saying they'll keep your credits.

Mina . . .

Mother   And we'll see what we can do about organising you another loan.

Mina   I've told you I hated university. I hated it.

Mother   Only recently. You were very, very happy the first year.

Mina   I hated it.

Pause.

Mother   You can't love everything in this world.

Mina   I know that.

Mother   And it would only be another two years.

Mina   . . .

Mother   It would be good for you.

Pause.

You'd get out a bit. (*Humouring* **Mina**. *Self-mocking*.) Stuck in here all the time you getting as old and fuddy-duddy as me. (*Pause*.) Worse even. You need to get out a bit.

Mina   . . .

Mother   It would be nice for you. (*Pause*.) I don't like seeing you always throwing yourself away with irresponsible rubbish.

Mina *shifts, irritated.*

Mother   You wasting yourself.

Pause.

Mina   I'm all right. I'm not a child any more.

Mother   I know that.

Pause.

Mina   So you don't have to tell me what to do or who I can or can't see.

Mother   . . .

Mina   And they my friends.

Mother   OK. You entitled to your opinion. I don't like them and I don't want them in my home. You can run around and do whatever you like but don't go trying to bring them into my home.

Mina   Did I say I wanted to?

Mother   I'm just telling you. I can hear it coming my girl. Whatever you do is your business but I don't want you bringing in that whole parasitic family with their begging bowl. No thank you. I don't like them and I don't want . . .

Mina   You've said that.

Mother   I'm just telling you.

Mina   I know.

Mother   Yes, all right you know. I'm just telling you.

Mina   OK.

Mother   OK, subject closed.

Long pause. **Mother** *stares at* **Mina**. *Uncomfortable. She perceives it as judgmental.*

Mina (*softly*)   You a real bitch, you know that.

Pause.

Mother (*hurt*)   You tell me you want me to stay with you. And now look at you.

Pause.

Mina   Well, look at you . . . (*Pause.*) Just leave me alone. Get out.

Mother   You a fool. A big fool. That's all, my girl. You might think you looking all p.c. but you a fool.

Mina   Get out.

Mother   You a fool. Go on run off with that boy . . .

Mina   Who?

Mother   That rubbish, I don't know, whatever his name is. You think I don't know?

Mina   Get out. Get out.

Mother   You think he loves you? Well, you wrong, he's using you, that's all. He's using you. My fat eye he loves you. My fat eye. He's after you for your money.

Mina   I don't have money.

Mother   You live in a house like this and you think to them you don't have money? You a joke. Go and open your legs, get yourself pregnant, get Aids, do whatever you like, I am not interested.

Mina   I will.

Mother   Ja, well good.

Mina (*screaming*)   Get the fuck out.

Mother   Don't you shout at me like that. You disgusting. You bloody disgusting. You treat me like I'm bloody filth. All right for your kaffir friends. But me you must treat me like filth. Anyone else it is fine. As long as someone else says it and it's p.c. enough for you, it's fine. But not me, nothing. Everything I do is wrong.

Long pause.

Everything.

Mina   That's not true.

Mother   Ag, you not interested in me. You think I'm stupid. You never want to hear my advice, my opinions.

Mina   I do.

Mother   Ja, look at you. Carrying on like this.

Mina   You just don't understand.

Mother   I understand. I've spent my whole life in this country. I was born here. My mother was born here. I understand.

Mina   It's not like that.

Mother   Do what you like. You are always against me. Even with your father. You were always siding with him. Running off to tell him one lie after another. Trying to drive him away from me.

Mina   No. I wanted him to come back. I would have done anything to have you together again.

Mother   . . .

Mina   I remember even sitting on the wall in the back garden. And making a pact with God. I needed blood to secure it. So I sat there burrowing with my toes in the sand and picking at my nails until they bled. (*Pause.*) And then you came and sat down next to me and put your arms around me and showed me that the tree at the bottom of the garden had suddenly grown pears.

Mother   Yes.

Mina   You remember?

Mother   Yes. And I knew then, that we didn't need him any more.

Mina   Yes.

Mother   Useless though. They so small and hard.

Mina   You promised that one day we could stew them. Or make jam.

Mother   Yes. Ag, we'll still do it one day when I have time. Maybe when we seventy-five and we so fat and old we can't even walk any more.

Mina   You. Not we.

Mother   Yes, yes, of course me. I'd hate that. Imagine, to see my baby old.

Mina   You won't.

Mother   Yes. Of course. I'll be dead and gone long before that.

Mina   Yes.

Pause.

Mother   All right, my baby, sleep. I must go. I'll be late. I'll be home this evening. We can talk more then.

Mina   I might not be here then.

Mother   All right, whatever. Then we'll talk tomorrow. Tonight, tomorrow, it's all the same thing. Just the two of us. The same – like always.

Scene Four

Sophie's *house. A crackly radio is playing.* **Mina** *sits at the table peeling potatoes.* **Sophie** *is sullen and angry.* **Mina** *is trying to be jovial in order to conceal the obvious tension.*

Sophie   Careful with that knife. You'll chop your paws off.

Mina   I won't.

Sophie   Nevertheless cut away from yourself. It's safer.

Mina   OK.

Sophie   Ja, I need an extra pair of arms – tomorrow for the shopping.

Mina   You want me to come?

Sophie   No. I want your arms to come. What do you think?

Mina   Chop them off. I hate shopping.

Sophie   If you want anything, put it on the list. But keep it small, you hear?

Mina   I don't need anything. Thanks.

Sophie   And you can ask Adele that too. To write down what she wants.

Mina   Shit. (*She cuts herself and sucks her hand.*)

Sophie   Aai! And now?

Mina   It was an accident. I swear. It wasn't deliberate.

Sophie   What have I just been telling you! Learn to cut away from you!!! Look at this! Wash your hands and put on a plaster. I'm not having you bleeding on the food.

Mina   It's OK.

Sophie   *Aikhona!* You wash that cut. Must I treat you like a child? (**Sophie** *pulls* **Mina** *and puts her hands under the tap.*) Here you are expecting yourself and you more of a child than ever. Go fetch a plaster. Look in that drawer.

Mina   There's nothing.

Sophie   You lazy to look. I also won't find anything if I look like that!

Mina   Stop fussing, Mama Sophie, it's OK.

Sophie   Aai, not OK. I'll have Adele refusing the food because she's acting strict vegetarian!

Mina   We can wash the potatoes again if it'll bother her. Or, I'll take out the one I was cutting and we can grow it. Remember, like we used to do with avocados.

Sophie   (*takes it away from* **Mina**, *rinses it and puts it back in the bowl*)   No, you leave that potato in peace, do all your planting and growing and what not back in your own mother's yard. Here.

She finds a plaster in the drawer and hands it to **Mina** *who puts it on.* **Adele** *enters. She is carrying a plastic carrier bag with papers, a tube of toothpaste and a toothbrush and other junk.*

Sophie   Close the door. Were you born in a stable that nobody taught you to close a door?

Adele   I picked it up like you asked on my way back from town.

Mina   Thanks.

Sophie   And now?

Adele   It's from her mother. (*To* **Mina**.) You should have gone yourself. She was very polite.

Mina   Really?

Adele   She couldn't not be, could she? But I think she wanted you to come. She said to tell you that you are to fetch the rest of the things you want by next week. Otherwise she is going to chuck them out.

Mina   Did she say anything else?

Adele   No . . . (*Hesitating.*)

Mina   What?

Adele   Nothing.

Mina   Look, she's even written my name on everything. As if she's scared someone will steal it.

Adele   How do you know?

Mina   I know her.

Adele   Maybe you wrong. Maybe she wanted you to know that it's yours.

Mina   Then she says that I must come clear out the rest of my stuff? I don't think so.

Sophie   You just don't want to think so.

Mina   I know her – she's my mother.

Sophie   No. You just too happy here – living off me. You can see she cares – See – she's sending you parcels! Next it will be letters! Long letters. You are going to get all your mail directed here! You are going to drive me mad with all your letters!!!

Mina (*matter of fact*) Nobody writes to me.

Sophie And now look at you! Take those feet off that chair! Parcels, letters, and now feet on the chair! You getting too comfortable. Like you lives here.

Mina I do live here.

Sophie (*snapping*) Are you going to stop that? The whole time, 'I live here', 'I do live here', 'This is my home here', 'Mama Sophie this, Mama Sophie that'. Not forever. Look what you talked me into, Adele! Your own mother wants you back and still you must stay here with me. The sooner you stop your nonsense and move out the better. It's not right me putting my son out to put up with the likes of you.

Sophie *continues cooking the supper.* **Mina** *peels the vegetables. Silence.*

Adele You not putting your son out.

Sophie And do you think he'll be here again with her in the house?

Adele And when was he here anyway?

Sophie Often. Often. And then soon it'll be the school holidays.

Mina I'll be gone by then.

Sophie Not at this rate you won't. At the rate you peeling – we won't have eaten by next Christmas, never you mind packed up and gone by the holidays. This is what I always get from you, Adele. Always. It would have been fine if you hadn't been poking your nose in every keyhole.

Pause.

You away all day – and she hides her face in here – but I'm the one who has to go outdoors – not you. I have to explain to everyone why I choose to put up with the likes of her.

Mina   If you don't want me, I'll go.

Sophie   It's not that I don't want you. It's just not forever.

Mina   I don't like this set up that much either.

Sophie   Oh, so now it's not good enough for her highness?

Mina   No. I am grateful. Very. But I'll find something else – for my child and me – don't worry. I also want to be gone.

Sophie   Your child. It's also our child.

Mina   We'll visit. Whenever he's not around.

Sophie   Haai. You know nothing. Look at these marks on them! You've make a useless job. I must teach you like a small child. And now you want him to have nothing with his child? Who's going to teach it when you so useless? The neighbours are always out laughing. The other day they were even laughing cos you doesn't even know the correct order to hang washing. They can't stop laughing not for one minute. And then they are demanding to know if the child will speak only English. They saying it's not right.

Adele   We can teach him.

Sophie   That's what I tell them – that already now it is listening to what we say whilst it's in her belly – and we are teaching him otherwise. But still that's what they want to know.

Mina   I want it to know other languages.

Sophie   Well, you can start yourself. Look at you, how long have you lived in this country – and still you don't understand one bloody word. I could tell you anything and you'd believe it.

Mina I'll learn.

Sophie Ag, you? The child will be fifty before you learn.

Pause. **Sophie** *starts clearing the table for supper.*

Sophie Tomorrow we doing the shopping. I need all the arms I can get.

Mina What time?

Adele I'm only free in the morning.

Sophie Then that's when we'll go. In the morning. Go and put this rubbish in the other room. And later – you call your mother. She might be worried about you.

Printed in the USA
CPSIA information can be obtained
at www.ICGtesting.com
LVHW041101171024
794057LV00001B/193